Enterprise React Development with UmiJS

Learn efficient techniques and best practices
to design and develop modern frontend
web applications

Douglas Alves Venancio

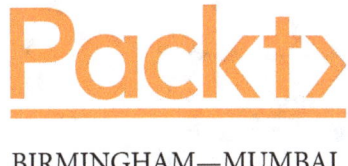

BIRMINGHAM—MUMBAI

Enterprise React Development with UmiJS

Associate Group Product Manager: Pavan Ramchandani

Publishing Product Manager: Aaron Tanna

Senior Editor: Aamir Ahmed

Content Development Editor: Rakhi Patel

Technical Editor: Saurabh Kadave

Copy Editor: Safis Editing

Project Coordinator: Manthan Patel

Proofreader: Safis Editing

Indexer: Hemangini Bari

Production Designer: Joshua Misquitta

Marketing Coordinater: Anamika Singh

First published: April 2022
Production reference: 1220422

Published by Packt Publishing Ltd.
Livery Place
35 Livery Street
Birmingham
B3 2PB, UK.
ISBN 978-1-80323-896-8
www.packt.com

I want to dedicate my work to my parents, Terezinha and Donisete, and my sisters Jemima and Elisama, for being by my side in the worst and best moments of my life, and all people who believed in me and are my family in Christ.

– Douglas Alves

Contributors

About the author

Douglas Alves Venancio has a background in systems analysis and development. His passion is to help customers and the community solve problems. Over the past few years, he has mainly worked with digital products and innovation, delivering the best user experience possible with modern web applications. Currently, Douglas works at the largest hospital in Latin America, innovating in telemedicine and digital transformation.

I want to pay my special regards to the entire team who worked with me on the success of this book and to Raul Oliveira for his valuable feedback!

I'd also like to express my gratitude to Teena Evans, who invested in me early in my career.

Finally, I would also like to thank my colleagues at AX4B for their support during the time we were together and to Albert Einstein Hospital and my co-workers for their support and for being part of my professional growth.

About the reviewer

Raul Oliveira is a developer with experience in frontend, backend, and robotic process automation. He has assisted in system integrations and the requirements gathering process and has architected, prototyped, developed, tested, and implemented enterprise solutions. He has particular experience in using React, Ant Design, UmiJS, Angular, Node, Java, Amazon Web Services, and SQL and NoSQL databases, among others. A graduate of systems analysis and development, he is curious about everything that involves technology and is always willing to help others.

Table of Contents

3

Using Models, Services, and Mocking Data

Part 2: Protecting, Testing, and Deploying Web Applications

4

Error Handling, Authentication, and Route Protection

5

Code Style and Formatting Tools

6

Testing Front-End Applications

7

Single-Page Application Deployment

Preface

UmiJS is a scalable JavaScript framework for building enterprise-level frontend applications. Umi uses React and is based on a routing system that allows you to make fast and responsive applications.

In this book, we will build a frontend web application for a **customer relationship management (CRM)** system. Starting with your environment setup, I will introduce you to the main features of UmiJS and how a project is structured. After that, we will explore Ant Design, a design system with a vast library of React components for quickly building modern and responsive user interfaces that deeply integrate with Umi.

You will also learn an approach based on models and services to handle HTTP requests and responses and control an application's state in complex scenarios.

After learning to work with Umi, you will explore how to improve code quality by implementing a consistent code style and using formatting tools such as Prettier and EditorConfig. You will also learn how to design and implement tests for frontend applications.

Finally, you will host your CRM frontend application on AWS Amplify, an out-of-the-box platform for frontend developers to build full-stack applications using several AWS services.

Who this book is for

This book is for React developers who are new to UmiJS and building large web applications. I assume you already know React and the basics of designing web applications.

What this book covers

Chapter 1, Environment Setup and Introduction to UmiJS, is where you will install all the tools you need to follow the exercises in this book and learn the main features of UmiJS.

Chapter 2, Creating User Interfaces with Ant Design, is where you will explore the Ant Design system and create interfaces using its React components library.

Chapter 3, Using Models, Services, and Mocking Data, is where you will learn an approach based on models and services to handle requests, manage application state, and simulate data using mock files.

Chapter 4, Error Handling, Authentication, and Route Protection, is where you will implement error handling, security controls, and authorization on your application.

Chapter 5, Code Style and Formatting Tools, is where we will discuss code style and configure Prettier and EditorConfig to automatically format and enforce a consistent code style in your project.

Chapter 6, Testing Front-End Applications, is where we will discuss software testing and implement some tests for your application using Puppeteer.

Chapter 7, Single-Page Application Deployment, is where you will prepare your application for deployment and host it on AWS Amplify.

To get the most out of this book

To complete these book exercises, you only need a computer with a modern operating system (such as Windows 10/11, macOS 10.15, or Ubuntu 20.04). I will give you instructions on how to install the other required software in *Chapter 1, Environment Setup and Introduction to UmiJS*.

Software/hardware covered in the book	Operating system requirements
Node.js v16.14.2	Windows, macOS, or Linux
Visual Studio Code v1.66.1	Windows, macOS, or Linux
Yarn v4.0.0	Windows, macOS, or Linux

It's important to mention that you will need a free GitHub account to access the code examples and to complete *Chapter 7, Single-Page Application Deployment*.

If you are using the digital version of this book, we advise you to type the code yourself or access the code from the book's GitHub repository (a link is available in the next section). Doing so will help you avoid any potential errors related to the copying and pasting of code.

Download the example code files

You can download the example code files for this book from GitHub at `https://github.com/PacktPublishing/Enterprise-React-Development-with-UmiJs`. If there's an update to the code, it will be updated in the GitHub repository.

We also have other code bundles from our rich catalog of books and videos available at `https://github.com/PacktPublishing/`. Check them out!

Conventions used

There are a number of text conventions used throughout this book.

`Code in text`: Indicates code words in text, database table names, folder names, filenames, file extensions, pathnames, dummy URLs, user input, and Twitter handles. Here is an example: "In this example, we used the `describe` method to create a group for two tests related to math problems."

A block of code is set as follows:

```
export default {
    'home.recents': 'Recent opportunities',
    'greetings.hello': 'Hello',
    'greetings.welcome': 'welcome',
};
```

When we wish to draw your attention to a particular part of a code block, the relevant lines or items are set in bold:

```
async function login(page: Page) {
    await page.goto('http://localhost:8000');
    await page.waitForNavigation();
    await page.type('#username', 'john@doe.com');
    await page.type('#password', 'user');
    await page.click('#loginbtn');
}
```

Any command-line input or output is written as follows:

```
yarn add -D puppeteer
```

Bold: Indicates a new term, an important word, or words that you see onscreen. For instance, words in menus or dialog boxes appear in **bold**. Here is an example: "The **Opportunities** page allows users to browse and register a new sale opportunity."

> **Tips or Important Notes**
> Appear like this.

Get in touch

Feedback from our readers is always welcome.

General feedback: If you have questions about any aspect of this book, email us at `customercare@packtpub.com` and mention the book title in the subject of your message.

Errata: Although we have taken every care to ensure the accuracy of our content, mistakes do happen. If you have found a mistake in this book, we would be grateful if you would report this to us. Please visit `www.packtpub.com/support/errata` and fill in the form.

Piracy: If you come across any illegal copies of our works in any form on the internet, we would be grateful if you would provide us with the location address or website name. Please contact us at `copyright@packt.com` with a link to the material.

If you are interested in becoming an author: If there is a topic that you have expertise in and you are interested in either writing or contributing to a book, please visit `authors.packtpub.com`.

Share your thoughts

Once you've read *Enterprise React Development with UmiJS*, we'd love to hear your thoughts! Scan the QR code below to go straight to the Amazon review page for this book and share your feedback.

https://packt.link/r/1803238968

Your review is important to us and the tech community and will help us make sure we're delivering excellent quality content.

Part 1: Configuring UmiJS and Creating User Interfaces

This section aims to introduce readers to UmiJS and explain its main features through practical examples. In this section, readers will create an Umi project from scratch, build interfaces, and manage the application state by implementing services and models.

This section comprises the following chapters:

- *Chapter 1, Environment Setup and Introduction to UmiJS*
- *Chapter 2, Creating User Interfaces with Ant Design*
- *Chapter 3, Using Models, Services, and Mocking Data*

1

Environment Setup and Introduction to UmiJS

UmiJS is Ant Financial's underlying frontend framework and an open source project for developing enterprise-class frontend applications. It's a robust framework you can combine with Ant Design to provide everything you need to build a modern user experience.

In this chapter, you will learn how to install and configure a project using UmiJS and **Visual Studio Code** (**VSCode**). You'll also understand the folder structure and main files of UmiJS. Then, you'll learn how to set fast navigation between pages using **umi history** and finally discover **Umi UI**, a visual option to interact with UmiJS and add components to your project.

We'll cover the following main topics:

- Setting up our environment and configuring UmiJS
- Understanding the UmiJS folder structure and its main files
- Exploring the Umi CLI and adding pages
- Understanding routing and navigation in UmiJS
- Using Umi UI

By the end of this chapter, you'll have learned everything you need to get started with developing your project and you will also know about the fundamental behavior of an UmiJS project and its configurations.

Technical requirements

To complete this chapter's exercises, you just need a computer with any OS (I recommend Ubuntu 20.04 or higher).

You can find the complete project in the Chapter01 folder in the GitHub repository available at the following link:

https://github.com/PacktPublishing/Enterprise-React-Development-with-UmiJs

Setting up our environment and configuring UmiJS

In this section, we'll install and configure VSCode, the EditorConfig extension, and the Prettier extension, and create our first UmiJS project.

Let's begin by installing a source code editor. You can use any editor that supports JavaScript and TypeScript, but I will use VSCode extensively in this book. It's a free editor with an integrated terminal and internal Git control that natively supports JavaScript, TypeScript, Node.js, and many extensions for other languages.

VSCode is available as a Snap package, and you can install it on Ubuntu by running the following command:

```
$ sudo snap install code --classic
```

For Mac users, you can install it using Homebrew on macOS by running the following command:

```
$ brew install --cask visual-studio-code
```

If you are using Chocolatey on Windows, you can run the following command:

```
> choco install vscode
```

Alternatively, you can download the installer available at `https://code.visualstudio.com/`.

> **Important Note**
>
> You can find instructions on installing **Homebrew** on macOS at `https://brew.sh/` and installing **Chocolatey** on Windows at `https://chocolatey.org/install`. If you are a Windows user, you can install Ubuntu in **Windows Subsystem for Linux** (**WSL**) and set up your project using common Linux commands. You can read more about WSL at `https://docs.microsoft.com/en-us/windows/wsl/install`.

Next, we need to install the dependencies required to develop with UmiJS. First, let's install Node.js by typing and running the following commands in the terminal:

```
$ sudo apt update
$ sudo apt install nodejs -y
```

The first command updates the mirrors, and the second command installs Node.js with the `-y` flag, which skips user confirmation to install.

You can install Node.js using Homebrew on macOS by running the following command:

```
$ brew install node
```

If you are using Chocolatey on Windows, you can run the following command:

```
> choco install nodejs
```

Alternatively, you can download the installer available at `https://nodejs.org/en/`.

Node.js has a default package manager named npm, but we will extensively use **Yarn** instead of npm in this book, so I recommend installing it. You can do that by running the following command in the terminal:

```
$ npm install -g yarn
```

This command will install Yarn globally in your system.

With that, we are ready to get started with UmiJS. But first, let's understand UmiJS a bit more and what kinds of problems it can solve.

Introduction to UmiJS and creating your first project

UmiJS is a framework for developing enterprise-class frontend applications. This means Umi provides a set of tools for solving everyday problems faced when building large business applications that need to deliver a modern user experience and must be easy to maintain and modify.

With Umi, you can quickly develop an application with internationalization, permissions, and beautiful interfaces taking advantage of Umi's deep integration with Ant Design.

Another significant advantage of Umi is that there are a variety of published plugins you can add to your project as you need. You can also extend it by developing your own plugins to meet specific solutions.

Now that you know more about Umi, let's create your first project by following these steps:

1. Create a new folder for the project and open it in the terminal:

    ```
    $ mkdir umi-app; cd umi-app
    ```

2. Create a new project using the umi-app template:

    ```
    $ yarn create @umijs/umi-app
    ```

3. Install the project dependencies by running the following command:

    ```
    $ yarn
    ```

4. Start the project by running the following command:

    ```
    $ yarn start
    ```

We now have a project set up! You can open it by typing http://localhost:8000 in the browser and see the result.

Let's do the final configurations to simplify our work by adding code formatting.

Installing the EditorConfig and Prettier extensions

One of the tools UmiJS provides by default in the umi-app template is **EditorConfig**, a file format that editors read to define the code style across IDEs and text editors. You'll learn more about code style in *Chapter 5, Code Style and Formatting Tools*. Some editors and IDEs offer native support to EditorConfig, while in other cases, such as VSCode, you need to install a plugin, so let's install it by following these steps:

1. Open VSCode and press *Ctrl + P*. This shortcut will open the following field at the top:

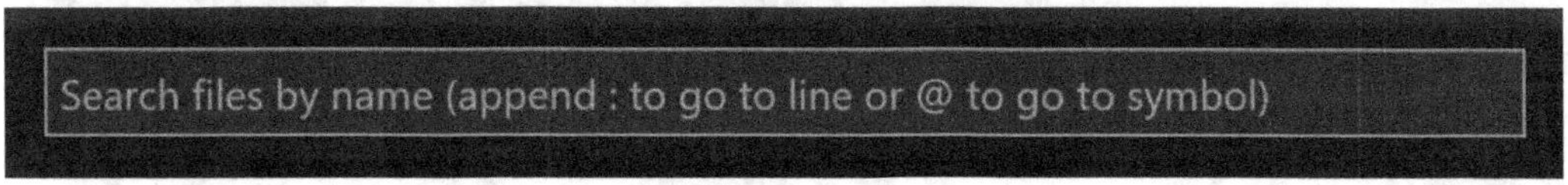

> Search files by name (append : to go to line or @ to go to symbol)

Figure 1.1 – VSCode quick open

2. Type the following command and press *Enter* to install the official extension for EditorConfig support:

```
ext install EditorConfig.EditorConfig
```

The umi-app template comes preinstalled with Prettier, which is preconfigured for formatting the code. You can use it by running the `yarn prettier` command. Still, a better option is to let VSCode format it for you when you save changes or paste code blocks.

For that, we need to install the Prettier extension and configure it as the default code formatter. To install and configure the Prettier extension, follow these steps:

1. Press *Ctrl + P* and type the following command, then press *Enter* to install the official extension for Prettier support:

```
ext install esbenp.prettier-vscode
```

2. Next, press *Ctrl + ,* to open the VSCode preferences, and in the search field, type `formatter` and press *Enter*.

3. Under **Editor: Default Formatter**, select **Prettier - Code formatter**.

4. Check the **Editor: Format On Paste** and **Editor: Format On Save** options, as shown in the following screenshot:

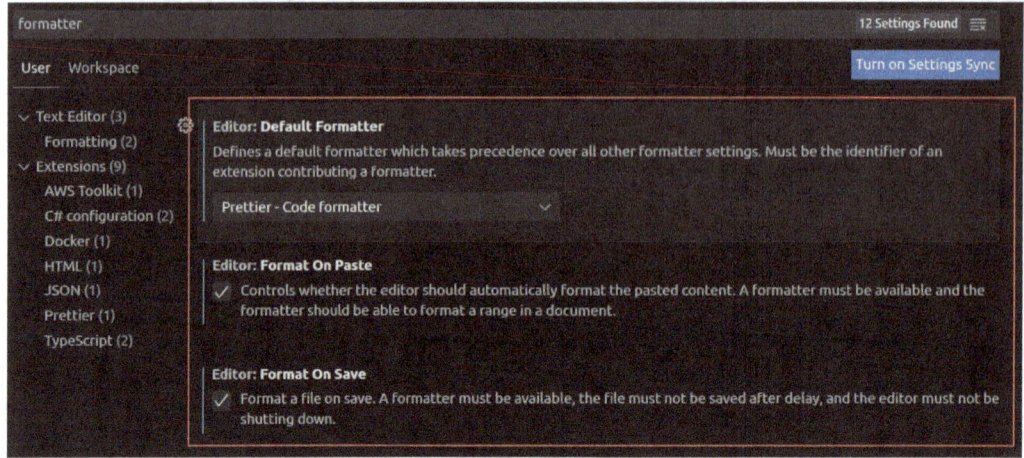

Figure 1.2 – VSCode editor configuration

In this section, we learned how to configure our environment, learned more about UmiJS, and created our first project. Now, let's take a closer look at the project structure.

Understanding the UmiJS folder structure and its main files

In this section, you will understand the UmiJS folder structure, and you will add some essential configurations to files and folders.

The project we create based on the umi-app template generates a set of folders with responsibilities for different parts of the project. Let's see what each one does:

- mock: In this folder, we store our simulated endpoints definitions to generate a mock API that we can interact with while developing the frontend.

- src: This is the source folder where all our components are located.

- src/.umi: This folder is automatically generated by UmiJS every time the project is compiled and contains its internal configurations.

- src/pages: The React components responsible for rendering the pages in response to configured routes are located in this folder.

These are the folders included with the umi-app template, but there are other essential folders in a UmiJS project, so let's add them.

The first folder we'll add is `config`.

Adding config and locales folders

In the root folder of our project, we have a file named `.umirc.ts`. This file contains the configuration for Umi and its plugins. When your project is compact, it's a good choice, but as it grows and becomes complex, the configuration file can become hard to maintain. To avoid that, we can break down our configuration into different parts located in the `config` folder. Let's do this now by opening your project in VSCode and following these steps:

1. In the root directory of your project, create a new folder named `config`.

    You can do that by clicking on the icon in the upper-right corner above the folders list.

Figure 1.3 – VSCode new folder icon

2. Move the `.umirc.ts` file to the `config` folder and rename it `config.ts`.

    You can rename a file by selecting it and pressing *F2*.

3. In the `config` folder, create a new file named `routes.ts`. In this file, we'll configure the application's routes.

    You can do that by clicking on the icon in the top-right corner, above the folders list.

Figure 1.4 – VSCode new file icon

4.   Paste this code into the `routes.ts` file and save:

```
export default [
  {
    path: '/',
    component: '@/pages/index',
  },
];
```

This code defines the root path (`'/'`) to render the component index located in the `pages` folder.

5.   Now we can import the `routes.ts` file into `config.ts` and add this line to the `config.ts` file:

```
import routes from './routes';
```

We can then rewrite the route section to use it as follows:

```
import { defineConfig } from 'umi';
import routes from './routes';

export default defineConfig({
  nodeModulesTransform: {
    type: 'none',
  },
  routes,
  fastRefresh: {},
});
```

Umi also supports **internationalization** (also known as **i18n**) through the **locale** plugin. You'll learn more about this and other helpful Umi plugins in later chapters. To enable internationalization, create a folder named `locales` in the `src` folder and add the following configuration to the `config.ts` file under the `config` folder:

---

config.ts

```
import { defineConfig } from 'umi';
import routes from './routes';
```

```
export default defineConfig({
  locale: {
    default: 'en-US',
    antd: true,
    baseNavigator: true,
    baseSeparator: '-',
  },
  nodeModulesTransform: {
    type: 'none',
  },
  routes,
  fastRefresh: {},
});
```

The `locale` configuration properties are as follows:

- `default`: The default application language.

- `antd`: Enable Ant Design components internationalization.

- `baseNavigator`: Enable browser language detection.

- `baseSeparator`: The separator used in multi-language files localized under the `src/locales` folder.

Now we can support internationalization by adding multi-language files in the `locales` folder. For example, to support the English language, we need to add a file named `en-US.js`.

Now, we'll add the `app.tsx` file to set configurations at runtime.

Runtime configuration

Umi uses a file named app.tsx to expand your application's configurations at runtime. This file is useful to configure the initial state using the **initial-state** plugin and the layout using the **layout** plugin. The app.tsx file needs to be located in the src folder.

Add a file named app.tsx to the src folder following the steps demonstrated previously.

At this point, our project structure should look like this:

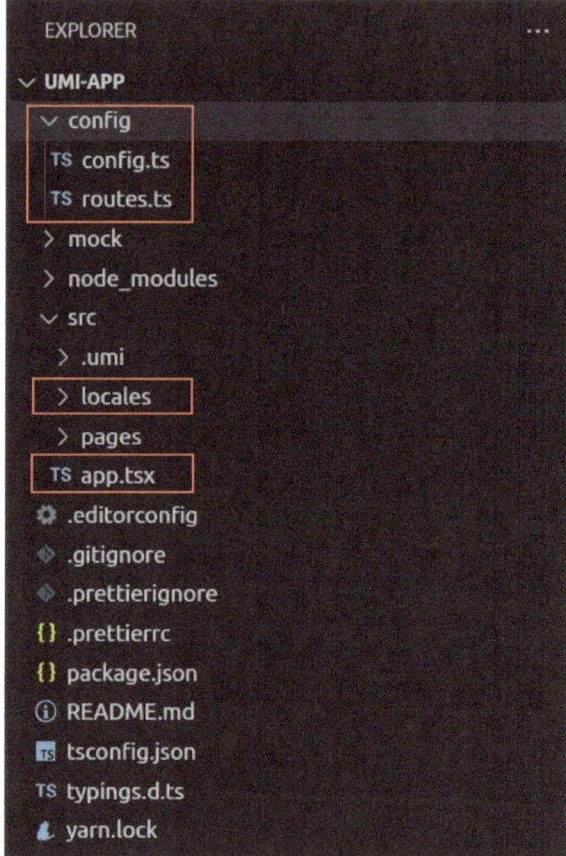

Figure 1.5 – Project structure after last modifications

You'll better understand all these features following the exercises in the upcoming chapters.

Now that you understand the Umi project structure and have added the missing folders and files, let's learn about some useful commands in the Umi **command-line interface (CLI)**.

Exploring the Umi CLI and adding pages

In this section, we'll explore the Umi CLI for automating tasks and use the `generate` command to add some pages to your project.

Umi provides a CLI with commands to build, debug, list configurations, and so on. You can use them to automate tasks. Some of these commands are already configured in the `umi-app` template as scripts in the `package.json` file: `yarn start` will execute `umi dev`, `yarn build` will execute `umi build`, and so on.

These are the main commands available:

- `umi dev`: Compiles the application and starts a development server for debugging.
- `umi build`: Compiles the application bundle in the `dist` folder.
- `umi webpack`: This shows the webpack configuration file generated by Umi.
- `umi plugin list`: Lists all Umi plugins in use.
- `umi generate page`: Creates a new page template.

> **Important Note**
>
> For more commands, refer to the documentation available at `https://umijs.org/docs/cli`.

Let's add some pages using the `generate page` Umi CLI command. Follow these steps:

1. First, delete the files under the `src/pages` folder, then add two pages by running these commands:

   ```
   $ yarn umi g page /Home/index --typescript --less
   $ yarn umi g page /Login/index --typescript --less
   ```

   These commands generate two components under the `pages` folder, `Login` and `Home`, with TypeScript and Less support.

2. To access these pages, we need to define routes, so modify your `routes.ts` file to define the created components for new routes:

routes.ts

```
export default [
  {
    path: '/',
```

```
        component: '@/pages/Login',
    },
    {
        path: '/home',
        component: '@/pages/Home',
    },
];
```

3. To check the result, start the project by running `yarn start`, then navigate to `http://localhost:8000/`; you should see the login page.

4. Navigate to `http://localhost:8000/home`; you should now see the home page.

Now that we have pages set up, we can learn more about Umi routing and navigation using umi history.

Understanding routing and navigation in UmiJS

In this section, you'll understand the Umi routing system and options for configuring routes. You will also learn how to access route parameters and query strings and about navigating between pages.

A Umi project is a **single-page application**. This means that the entire application remains on the first page served to the browser (`index.html`), and all other pages we see when accessing different addresses are components rendered on this same page. Umi does the job of parsing the route and rendering the correct component; we just need to define which component to render when the route matches a specific path. As you may have noticed, we already did that. But there are other configuration options. For example, we can set subroutes to define a standard layout for various pages:

routes.ts

```
export default [
    {
        path: '/',
        component: '@/layouts/Header',
        routes: [
            { path: '/login', component: '@/pages/Login' },
```

```
        { path: '/home', component: '@/pages/Home' },
    ],
  },
];
```

The preceding example defines that all routes under ' / ' will have a default header, which is a component located in the `src/layouts` folder.

The header component should look like this:

```
import React from 'react';
import styles from './index.less';

export default function (props: { children: React.ReactChild })
{
  return (
    <div className={styles.layout}>
      <header className={styles.header}>
        <h1>Umi App</h1>
      </header>
      {props.children}
    </div>
  );
}
```

`props.children` will receive the components when you access a defined route.

Another option we have is to redirect routes. Consider the following example:

routes.ts

```
export default [
  {
    path: '/',
    redirect: '/app/login',
  },
  {
    path: '/app',
    component: '@/layouts/Header',
```

```
  routes: [
    { path: '/app/login', component: '@/pages/Login' },
    { path: '/app/home', component: '@/pages/Home' },
  ],
 },
];
```

With this configuration, when you access `http://localhost:8000/`, Umi will immediately redirect the page to `http://localhost:8000/app/login`.

We can also define whether a path should be exact or not:

```
{
    exact: false,
    path: '/app/login',
    component: '@/pages/Login',
}
```

This configuration defines that you can access this page in any path under `/app/login`, such as `http://localhost:8000/app/login/user`. By default, all paths are exact.

You now understand how the routing system works and the different configuration options we have for routing. Now, you will learn how to access path and query string parameters and about conventional routing and navigating between pages.

Understanding path parameters and query strings

Sometimes we need to identify a resource in the route path. Imagine we have a page in our project that only displays product information. When accessing this page, we need to specify what product to get information from. We can do that by identifying the product ID in the route path:

```
{
    path: '/product/:id',
    component: '@/pages/Product',
},
```

If the parameter is not mandatory to access the page, you must add the ? character, like this: `/product/:id?`.

To access the product ID, we can use the `useParams` hook provided by Umi:

```
import { useParams } from 'umi';


export default function Page() {
  const { id } = useParams<{ id: string }>();
```

You can also receive query string parameters after the route. Query string parameters are key-value pairs in the `?` character sequence in a URL, such as this example: `/app/home?code=eyJhbGci`. Here, `code` contains the value `eyJhbGci`.

We don't have a specific hook to access query string parameter values, but we can easily do that using umi history:

```
import { history } from 'umi';


export default function Page() {
  const { query } = history.location;
  const { code } = query as { code: string };
```

Now, let's see how you can define parameters when working with conventional routing.

Conventional routing

UmiJS offers an automatic route configuration based on your project structure under the `pages` folder. UmiJS will rely on that if it can't find route definitions in the `config.ts` or `.umirc.ts` files.

If you want to configure a route parameter, you can name the file enclosed in `[]`, like this: `[id].tsx`. If this parameter is not mandatory to access the page, you must add the `$` character, like this: `[id$].tsx`.

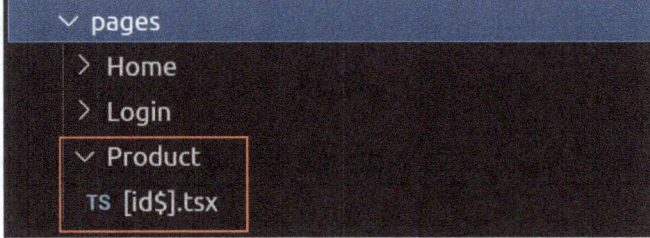

Figure 1.6 – Optional route parameter in conventional routing

Next, you will see how to navigate between pages.

Navigating between pages

When we need to set navigation between pages, usually, we use the DOM history object and anchor tag. In UmiJS, we have similar options to navigate: **umi history** and the `Link` component.

You can create hyperlinks between pages using the `Link` component, as in the following example:

```
import { Link } from 'umi';

export default function Page() {
  return (
    <div>
      <Link to="/app/home">Go Home</Link>
    </div>
  );
}
```

You can also set navigation between pages using the `push()` umi history command, as in the following example:

```
import { history } from 'umi';

export default function Page() {
  const goHome = () => {
    history.push('/app/home');
  };

  return (
    <div>
      <button onClick={goHome}></button>
    </div>
  );
}
```

In addition to the push() command, umi history has the goBack() command to revert one page in the history stack and goForward() to advance one page.

We have covered all the essential aspects of the Umi routing system, the different options to configure routes, access path and query string parameters, and navigation between pages.

Before finishing this chapter, I will introduce an exciting feature Umi provides if you prefer to interact with the project visually.

Using Umi UI

Umi UI is a visual extension of Umi to interact with the project. You can run commands to install dependencies, verify and test code, build the project, and add components through a graphical user interface.

Before using Umi UI, we need to add the @umijs/preset-ui package. You can do that by running the following command:

```
$ yarn add @umijs/preset-ui -D
```

Now, when you start the project, you should see the following console log:

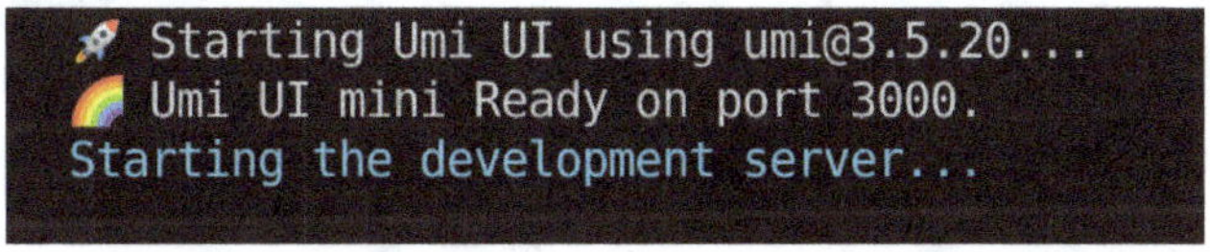

Figure 1.7 – Umi UI starting log

Navigate to `http://localhost:8000`, and you will notice that the UmiJS logo appears in a bubble in the bottom-right corner. Clicking on this bubble will open Umi UI (you can also access Umi UI at `http://localhost:3000`).

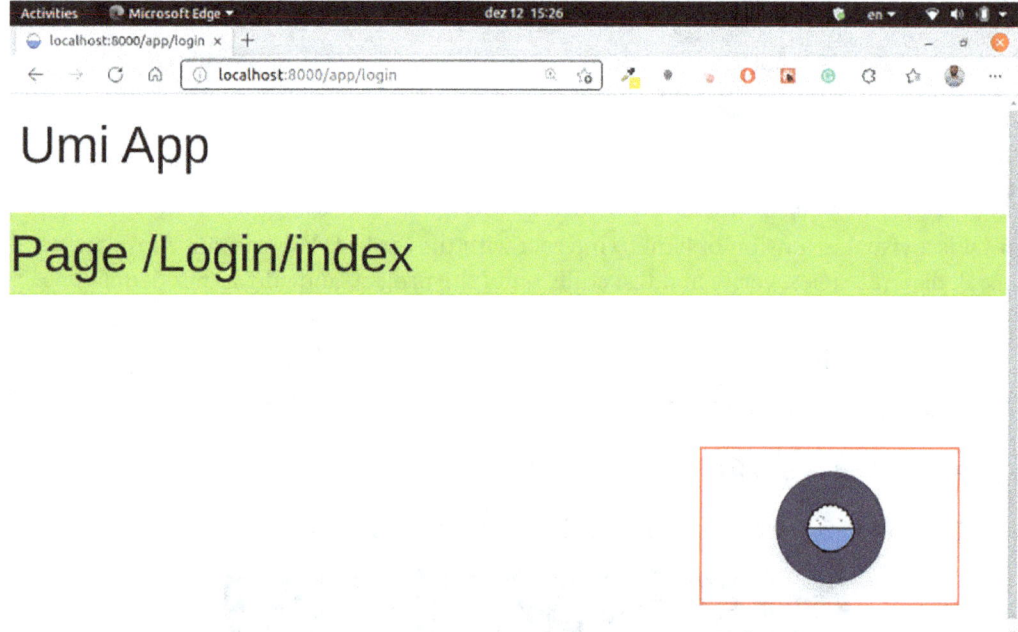

Figure 1.8 – Umi UI bubble in the bottom-right corner

Let's see what we can do using Umi UI, beginning with **tasks**:

- **BUILD**: This option will create the application bundle in the `dist` folder. You can also click on **ENVS** to select compilation options, such as CSS compression.

- **LINT**: This option will execute linters in your project. You need to configure the `lint` script to use this option.

- **TEST**: This option will test the project. You need to write tests first.

- **INSTALL**: This option will install all project dependencies.

The following screenshot shows the Umi UI Task tab:

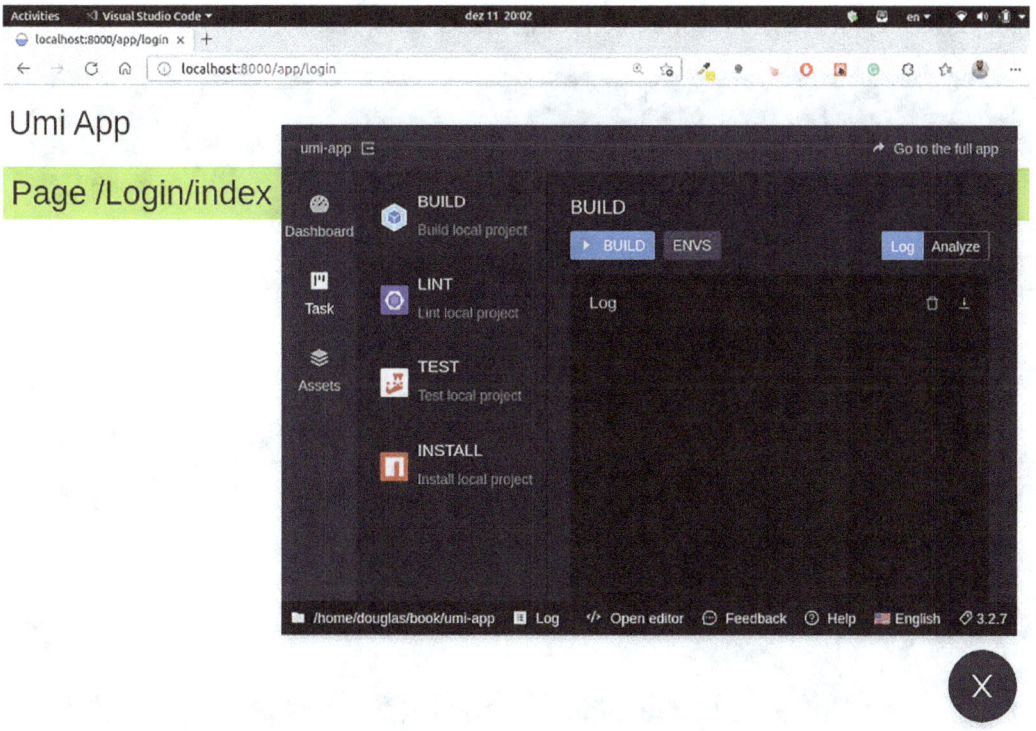

Figure 1.9 – Umi UI Task tab

Next, let's add Ant Design components to our project.

Adding Ant Design components

Ant Design is a design system created by Ant Financial's user experience design team to meet the high demands of enterprise application development and fast changes in these applications. They also created a React UI library of components for building interfaces.

In the **Assets** tab, we can add Ant Design components to our pages as blocks:

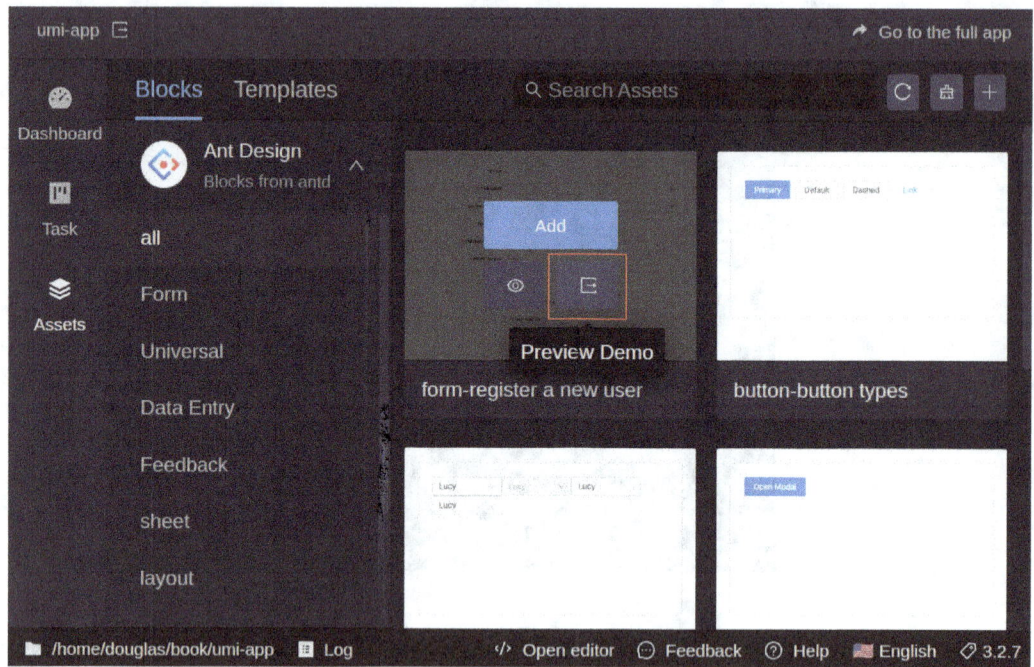

Figure 1.10 – Umi UI Preview Demo button

> **Tip**
>
> The Umi UI **Assets** tab is almost entirely in Chinese at the moment. Still, you can always refer to the Ant Design documentation by clicking on **Preview Demo** and changing the website language to English.

Let's add a login form to experiment with this feature:

1. Navigate to `http://localhost:8000` and open the Umi UI **Assets** tab.
2. Click on **Add** in the **form-login box** component.

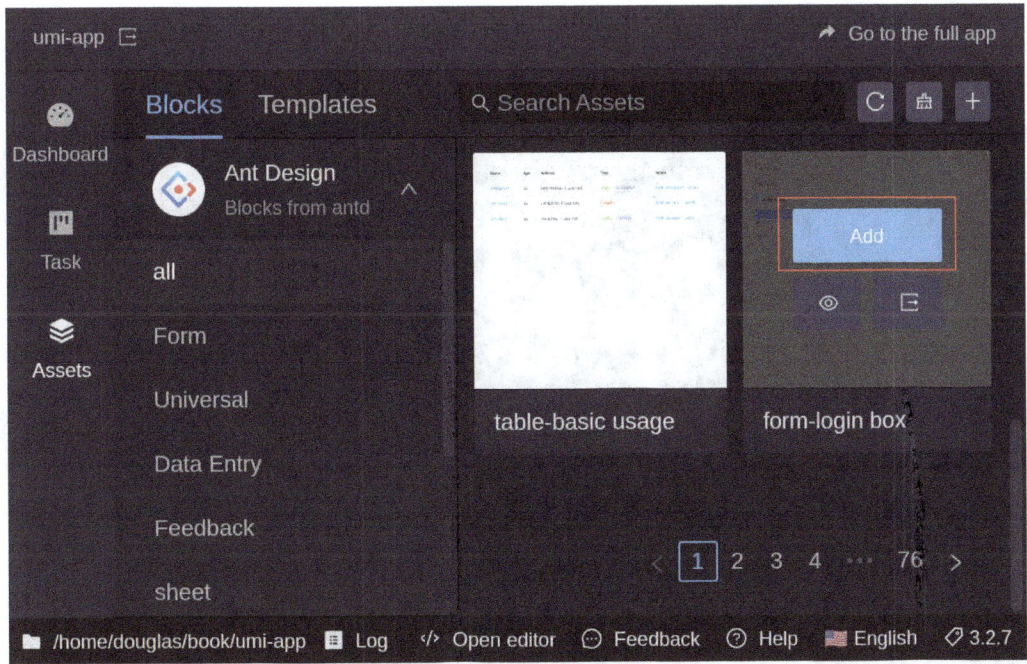

Figure 1.11 – form-login box component Add button

3.   Select the second area by clicking on + **Add to here**.

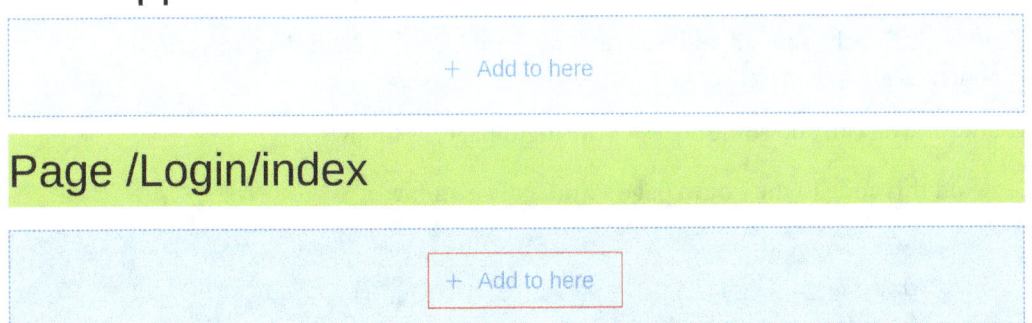

Figure 1.12 – Selecting where to add the component

4. Now, in the **Variable Name** field, type `LoginForm`, make sure the package manager client selected is **yarn**, and click on **OK**.

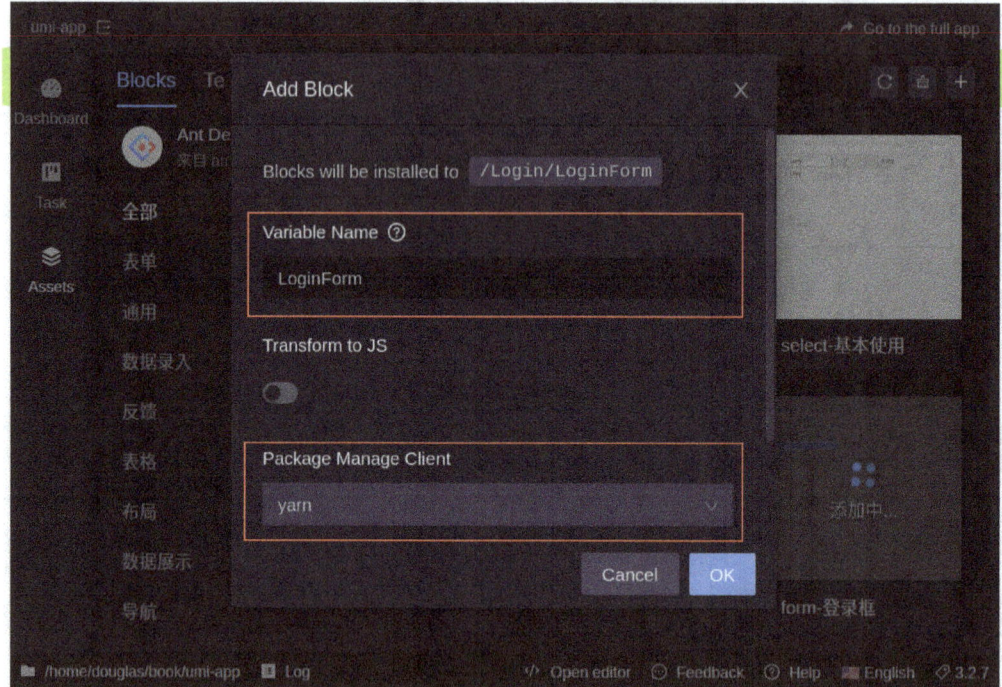

Figure 1.13 – Add Block options

Wait until the block is added and we are done. Umi UI will reload the page, and the component is already there!

If you want, you can add some styles to the login page, as follows:

1. Add this code to the **Login** page's `index.less` file:

```
.container {
    display: flex;
    flex-direction: column;
    align-items: center;
}
```

2. Add the `container` CSS class to the login component:

```
import React from 'react';
import styles from './index.less';
```

```
import LoginForm from './LoginForm';

export default function Page() {
  return (
    <div className={styles.container}>
      <h1 className={styles.title}>
        Welcome! Access your account.</h1>
      <LoginForm />
    </div>
  );
}
```

The result should look like this:

Umi App

Welcome! Access your account.

 Username

 Password

✔ Remember me Forgot password

Log in
Or register now!

Figure 1.14 – Login page with login form block

And that's it! Now you know how to use Umi UI to interact with your project. If you like this option, I recommend experimenting with it by adding more components and styling them to get you used to it.

Summary

In this chapter, you learned how to configure VSCode to work with UmiJS. You learned how to set up a project and organize the UmiJS folder structure. You also learned how to use the Umi CLI to automate tasks and quickly add pages and templates to your project.

You learned that an UmiJS project is a single-page application and about various configurations to define routes in your project. You learned how to access path parameters and query string parameters. You also learned how UmiJS could automatically configure routes based on the folder convention. You learned about navigation using umi history and the link component.

Finally, you learned how to install and use Umi UI to interact with your project. You then learned how to execute tasks using Umi UI and add Ant Design components as blocks in your project.

In the next chapter, you will learn more about Ant Design in a Umi project and how to use it to develop interfaces.

2
Creating User Interfaces with Ant Design

Following the principles of **Ant Design**, the Ant Financial user experience design team created the antd library, which offers a variety of React components you can use to accelerate user interface development.

In this chapter, we'll study the antd library and create user interfaces using it. The first section will introduce you to the project we will develop, a **Customer Relationship Management (CRM)** application. Then, we'll configure the layout plugin and theme. We'll create the home page and configure internationalization support (also known as **i18n**). Finally, we'll make the **Opportunities** page, **Customers** page, and **Reports** page.

In this chapter, we'll cover the following main topics:

- Introduction to the project and Ant Design
- Setting up the layout and theme
- Creating the home page and setting up i18n
- Creating the Opportunities and Customers pages
- Creating the **Reports** page

By the end of this chapter, you'll have learned how to search and find the right component to meet your needs in the `antd` library. You'll have learned how to configure `plugin-layout`, customize your application's default theme, and define global styles. You'll also know how to set up support for internationalization using `plugin-locale`.

Technical requirements

To complete this chapter's exercises, you only need a computer with any OS (I recommend Ubuntu 20.04 or higher) and the software installed in *Chapter 1, Environment Setup and Introduction to UmiJS* (VScode, Node.js, and Yarn).

You can find the complete project in the `Chapter02` folder on the GitHub repository available at:

`https://github.com/PacktPublishing/Enterprise-React-Development-with-UmiJs`

Introduction to the project and Ant Design

This section will introduce you to the project we'll develop and the Ant Design React library.

To illustrate the real-world use of UmiJS and Ant Design, we'll develop a frontend application for a CRM system.

A CRM system is a business application that allows a company to approach a customer, offer a solution, and develop a relationship with various strategic contacts to sell the right solution to the customer and guarantee their satisfaction.

In our example, the application has three main features: a dashboard with various reports, a registry tracking opportunities, and a registry of customers.

We'll also guarantee that our application is easy to be extended and modified in the face of business requirements, has a clean code style, and supports internationalization.

To build the interfaces of our frontend application, we'll use the Ant Design React library. Let's learn more about the `antd` library and the Pro components.

Introduction to Ant Design components

The Ant Design library is a React components library created following the design principles of the Ant Design system. The Ant Design library was written in TypeScript and offers predictable static types, internationalization support, and theme customization. The library is also deeply integrated with UmiJS, so it's easy to customize the theme and set internationalization support using it with UmiJS.

You can browse the library and look for components at `https://ant.design/components/overview/`. On this documentation page, you will find detailed descriptions of every library component and use case examples followed by their respective code.

We'll also use some components from **Pro components**, a set of components derived from Ant Design, to provide a high level of abstraction, making the task of building complex interfaces easier. You can look for Pro components at `https://procomponents.ant.design/en-US/components`.

In this section, you learned about the Ant Design React library and were introduced to the project we will build. Let's start building the interfaces by setting the default layout and theme.

Setting up the layout and theme

In this section, we'll set up a default layout using `plugin-layout` and customize our application theme, changing the default LESS variables used by `antd`. To do that, follow these steps:

1. We'll use the project we created in the previous chapter. Add the `plugin-layout` configuration to the `config.ts` file as follows:

```
layout: {
    navTheme: 'light',
    layout: 'mix',
    contentWidth: 'fluid',
    fixedHeader: false,
    fixSiderbar: true,
    colorWeak: false,
    title: 'Umi CRM',
```

```
    locale: true,
    pwa: false,
    logo: 'https://img.icons8.com/ios-filled/50/ffffff/
        customer-insight.png',
    iconfontUrl: '',
},
```

This configuration adds a page header and a menu for all pages, defines the application name and logo, and enables `plugin-locale` in layout components.

You can also change the layout as you need. For example, you can set the menu to appear in the header instead of a side menu, changing the `layout` property to `top`.

2. Let's also change the primary color that all interfaces and components use. Add this configuration to the `config.ts` file:

```
theme: {
    'primary-color': '#1895bb',
},
```

The theme configuration changes the default values of LESS variables used by Ant Design components.

> **Important Information**
>
> You can find all the default LESS variables at `https://github.com/ant-design/ant-design/blob/master/components/style/themes/default.less`.

3. Next, we need to add some configurations for `plugin-layout` in the `app.tsx` file. Add the following to the `app.tsx` file:

```
import routes from '../config/routes';
import { RunTimeLayoutConfig } from 'umi';

export const layout: RunTimeLayoutConfig = () => {
  return {
    routes,
    rightContentRender: () => <></>,
    onPageChange: () => {},
  };
};
```

With this configuration, we set the routes `plugin-layout` that will render on the side menu.

4. To display menu items correctly in the side menu, adjust the route configuration as follows:

routes.ts

```
export default [
  {
    path: '/login',
    component: '@/pages/Login',
    layout: false,
  },
  {
    path: '/',
    name: 'home',
    icon: 'home',
    component: '@/pages/Home',
  },
];
```

We defined the routes to the login page and the home page. The `layout: false` property will make the default layout not appear on the login page. The `name` and `icon` properties define how the `Home` page will appear on the side menu.

Ant Design provides the icon, and you can look for other icons at `https://ant.design/components/icon/`.

Now let's finish our default layout by adding a quick menu, a language selector, and changing its style to use our primary color.

Adding right-side content to the layout header

First, let's create two new components: `HeaderMenu`, which will contain the user's avatar, the user's name, and the logout menu item; and the `HeaderOptions` component, which will include the `HeaderMenu` and the `SelectLang` components. `SelectLang` is a component provided by UmiJS to change between languages supported by the application through `plugin-locale`.

Follow these steps to create the `HeaderMenu` component:

1. Create a new folder named `components` in the `src` folder and inside it, create a new folder named `HeaderMenu`.

2. In the `HeaderMenu` folder, create two files: `index.tsx` and `index.less`.

3. In the `index.tsx` file, create the component as follows:

```tsx
import { Avatar, Dropdown, Menu } from 'antd';
import styles from './index.less';
import { LogoutOutlined } from '@ant-design/icons';


export default function HeaderMenu() {
  const options = (
    <Menu className={styles.menu}>
      <Menu.Item key="center">
        <LogoutOutlined /> Logout
      </Menu.Item>
    </Menu>
  );


  return (
    <Dropdown
      className={styles.dropdown}
      overlay={options}>
      <span>
        <Avatar
          size="small"
          className={styles.avatar} />
        <span
          className={`${styles.name} anticon`}>
          John Doe
```

```
        </span>
      </span>
    </Dropdown>
  );
}
```

In this component, we use the `antd` library `Menu` component to render the logout menu item and the `Dropdown` and `Avatar` components to render the user's avatar and the user's name. The logout option will appear when you mouse over the username or avatar.

4. Create the CSS classes for the `Avatar` and `Dropdown` components in the `index. less` file as follows:

```less
.avatar {
  color: white;
  background-color: #1895bb;
  margin: 0px 10px;
}

.dropdown {
  display: flex;
  flex-flow: row nowrap;
  cursor: pointer;
  align-items: center;
  float: right;
  height: 48px;
  margin-left: auto;
  overflow: hidden;
}
```

Now follow these steps to create the `HeaderOptions` component:

1. In the `components` folder, create a new folder named `HeaderOptions`. Inside it, create a file called `index.tsx`.

2. In the `index.tsx` file, create the component as follows:

```tsx
import { Space } from 'antd';
import { SelectLang } from 'umi';
import HeaderMenu from '../HeaderMenu';
```

```
export default function HeaderOptions() {
  return (
    <Space>
      <HeaderMenu />
      <SelectLang />
    </Space>
  );
}
```

In this component, we use the Space component of antd and the recently created HeaderMenu component with the SelectLang component from UmiJS to render the layout header options.

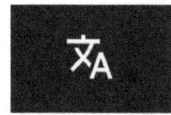

Figure 2.1 – The language selector (SelectLang component)

Now, to add the HeaderOptions component to the layout, follow these steps:

1. Import the HeaderOptions component, adding this line to the app.tsx file:

```
import HeaderOptions from './components/HeaderOptions';
```

2. Add the HeaderOptions component to the rightContentRender configuration as follows:

```
export const layout: RunTimeLayoutConfig = () => {
  return {
    routes,
    rightContentRender: () => <HeaderOptions />,
    onPageChange: () => {},
  };
};
```

Now the `HeaderOptions` component should appear in the layout header as follows:

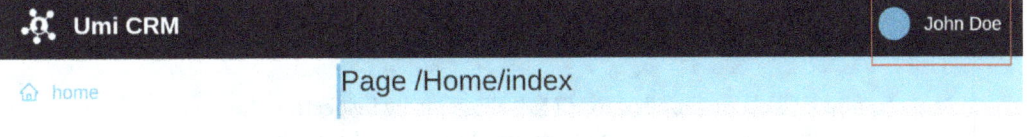

Figure 2.2 – Layout right content

You may have noticed that the language selector did not appear. It will appear once we add language support to the project.

To finish setting up our layout, let's add the primary color. We can customize the CSS class applied to the layout header using the `global.less` file to add the primary color.

UmiJS will apply the `global.less` file before all other style sheets, so when you need to customize some style or apply it across all interfaces, you can do that using this file.

Follow these steps to customize the CSS class applied to the layout header:

1. Create a new file under the `src` folder named `global.less`.

2. Add this style to the `global.less` file:

```less
.ant-pro-global-header-layout-mix {
    background: #1895bb;
    background: linear-gradient(50deg, #1895bb 0%,
        #14cfbd 100%);
}
```

We added a background gradient using our primary color to the CSS class and applied that to the global header.

> **Tip**
>
> You can find CSS classes applied to HTML elements by inspecting the page with your browser dev tools. Usually, you need to press *F12* and look for the **Elements** tab.

Now the layout header should look like this:

Figure 2.3 – Layout header with primary color applied

In this section, we set up the default layout for all pages by configuring `plugin-layout` and customizing the layout using the `global.less` file. We also created the components to render the user's avatar, the user's name, and the language selector. Now let's build the home page and set up internationalization.

Creating the home page and setting up i18n

In this section, we'll create the home page and set up the application's internationalization for Portuguese and English.

Our home page will be composed of two main components: `PageContainer` and `ProTable`. When users log in to the application, we want them to see some information such as the user's name, role, and a list of recently opened opportunities. To do that, follow these steps:

1. Let's start by adding the `PageContainer` component to the `index.tsx` file under the `src/pages/Home` folder as follows:

```tsx
import styles from './index.less';
import { PageContainer } from '@ant-design/pro-layout';
import { UserOutlined } from '@ant-design/icons';

export default function IndexPage() {
  return (
    <PageContainer
      header={{ title: undefined }}
```

```
        style={{ minHeight: '90vh' }}
        content={<></>}
    ></PageContainer>
    );
}
```

By default, the `PageContainer` component will render the page title you defined as the route name in the `routes.ts` file, but we set it to `undefined` as we don't want to display the title on this page.

2. Now we'll add some basic information to the content of `PageContainer`. We want it so that when the user logs into the application, they see a greeting followed by their name, role, and avatar, so go ahead and add the following information to the `content` property of `PageContainer` as follows:

```
content={
<div className={styles.pageHeaderContent}>
        <div className={styles.avatar}>
        <Avatar
            alt="avatar"
            className={styles.avatarComponent}
            size={{ xs: 64, sm: 64, md: 64, lg: 64,
            xl: 80, xxl: 100 }}
            icon={<UserOutlined />}
        />
        </div>
        <div className={styles.content}>
        <div className={styles.contentTitle}>
        Hello John Doe, welcome.</div>
        <div>Inside Sales | Umi Group</div>
        </div>
</div>
    }
```

Here, we added the `Avatar` component from `antd` followed by the greeting, the user's name, and role.

3. We also need to define the styles in the file index.less. Add these styles to the
    index.less file under the src/pages/Home folder as follows:

```less
@import '~antd/es/style/themes/default.less';

.pageHeaderContent {
  display: flex;

  .avatar {
    flex: 0 1 72px;
    & > span {
      display: block;
      width: 72px;
      height: 72px;
      border-radius: 72px;
    }

    .avatarComponent {
      color: white;
      background-color: @primary-color;
    }
  }

  .content {
    position: relative;
    top: 4px;
    flex: 1 1 auto;
    margin-left: 24px;
    color: @text-color-secondary;
    line-height: 22px;

    .contentTitle {
      margin-bottom: 12px;
      color: @heading-color;
      font-weight: 500;
      font-size: 20px;
      line-height: 28px;
```

```
        }
      }
    }
```

Notice that we imported a file called `default.less` from antd. This file contains the default LESS variables used by Ant Design components to define the styles. We are using some of these variables in our CSS classes too.

I highly recommend you familiarize yourself with these variables; this will help you maintain a consistent style with the Ant Design specification. You can access the `default.less` file by pressing *Ctrl* and clicking on its import path, or you can see the file on GitHub at `https://github.com/ant-design/ant-design/blob/master/components/style/themes/default.less`.

The next component we'll add to our page is `ProTable`; this is a Pro components component that abstracts the logic for manipulating a batch of data in a table.

4. To add the component, we need to install its package, so run this command to do so:

```
$ yarn add @ant-design/pro-table
```

5. Next, add the `ProTable` component inside the `PageContainer` component in the `index.tsx` file under `src/pages/Home` as follows:

```
<div style={{ width: '100%' }}>
  <ProTable<any>
    headerTitle="Recent opportunities"
    pagination={{ pageSize: 5 }}
    rowKey="id"
    search={false}
  />
</div>
```

At this point, your home page should look like this:

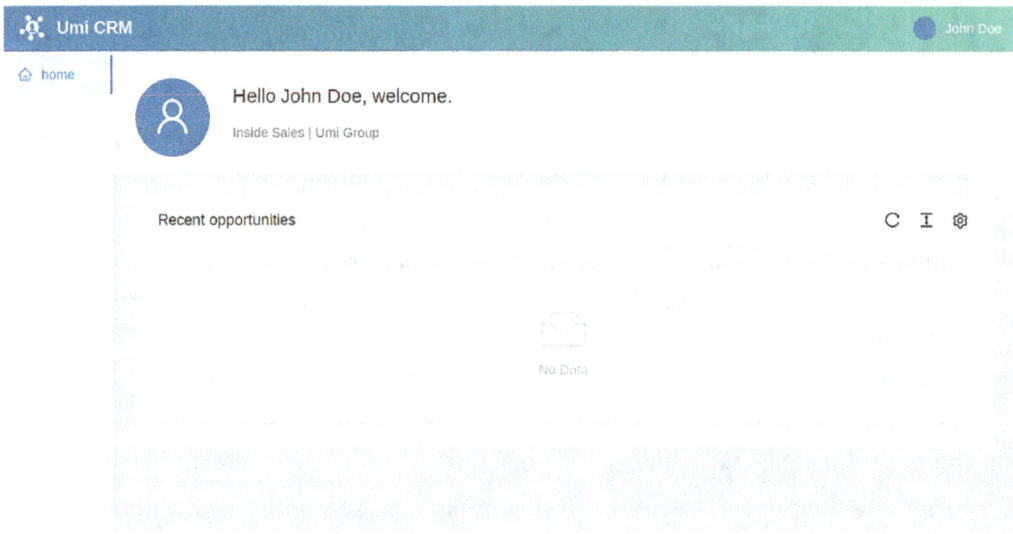

Figure 2.4 – Home page interface

Now it's time to add support for **internationalization (i18n)** to our application.

Setting up internationalization

To add support to i18n using `plugin-locale`, first, we must move all the text we want to translate to multi-language files under the `src/locales` folder. I'll build the entire application in English and Portuguese to demonstrate this feature, but you don't need to worry about it; you can download the Portuguese files available at `https://github.com/PacktPublishing/Enterprise-React-Development-with-UmiJs`. Follow these steps to create our language files:

1. Create a file named `en-US.ts` under the `src/locales` folder, download the file `pt-BR.ts`, and place it under the same folder.

2. Type the texts for the home page in the `en-US.ts` file as follows:

```
export default {
    'home.recents': 'Recent opportunities',
    'greetings.hello': 'Hello',
    'greetings.welcome': 'welcome',
};
```

3. We need to change the texts on the home page with the `FormattedMessage` component. Import the component in the `index.ts` file under the `src/pages` folder, adding this line:

```
import { FormattedMessage } from 'umi';
```

4. And change the text of the component as follows:

```
<div className={styles.content}>
    <div className={styles.contentTitle}>
        <FormattedMessage id="greetings.hello" />
        John Doe, {' '}
        <FormattedMessage id="greetings.welcome" />.
    </div>
    <div>Inside Sales | Umi Group</div>
</div>
```

5. Also change the `ProTable` `headerTitle` property as follows:

```
headerTitle={<FormattedMessage id="home.recents" />}
```

The `FormattedMessage` component property `id` must match the same key in the `en-US.ts` and the `pt-BR.ts` files. As you select the language, the component will render the corresponding text.

We want the menu titles translated, so let's add files to translate menu items. Follow these steps:

1. Create a new folder named `en-US` under the `src/locales` folder. Under the `en-US` folder, create a new file named `menu.ts`.

2. Add the text to render in the menu item to the `menu.ts` file as follows:

```
export default {
  'menu.home': 'Home',
};
```

The key for the text needs to match the `name` property in the `routes.ts` file. `plugin-locale` will render the correct text as you change between languages.

3. Import the `menu.ts` file into the `en-US.ts` file as follows:

```
import menu from './en-US/menu';

export default {
```

```
    ...menu,
    'home.recents': 'Recent opportunities',
    'greetings.hello': 'Hello',
    'greetings.welcome': 'welcome',
};
```

4. We also need to add the menu.ts file to the Portuguese language, so create a new folder named pt-BR, under the src/locales folder, download the menu.ts file available at https://github.com/PacktPublishing/Enterprise-React-Development-with-UmiJs, and place it under the pt-BR folder.

Now you can change the application's language using the language selector at the top of the page, as shown in the following screenshot:

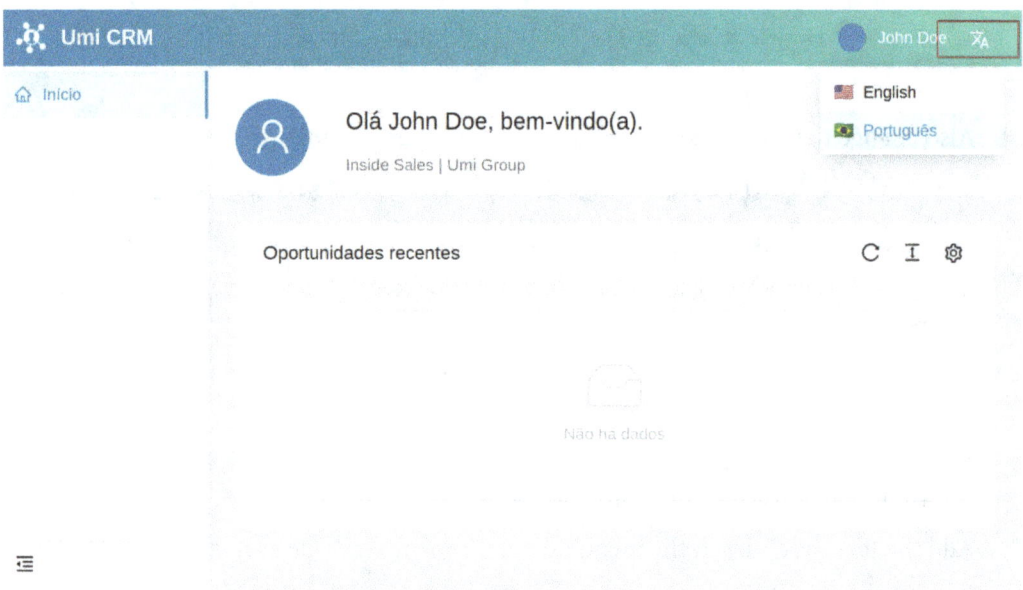

Figure 2.5 – Home page with the Portuguese language selected

In this section, we created the home page using the PageContainer and ProTable components. We also set up internationalization by creating multi-language files under the src/locales folder and using the FormattedMessage component to replace the texts with their corresponding translations.

Now, you'll use what you learned to create the **Opportunities** and **Customers** pages.

Creating the Opportunities and Customers pages

In this section, we'll build the **Opportunities** and **Customers** pages.

The **Opportunities** page allows users to browse and register a new sale opportunity. A sale opportunity occurs when a customer seems interested in buying a product or service. On the **Opportunities** page, we track all activities performed until the opportunity is won, when the customer buys the product or service, or until the opportunity is lost, when the customer buys a competitor's product or withdraws from the purchase.

The **Customers** page allows users to register and search for customers' contact information.

These two pages are similar; they use the `ProTable` component to list the opportunities and customers registered. Run the following commands to generate the two pages:

```
$ yarn umi g page /Customers/index --typescript --less
$ yarn umi g page /Opportunities/index --typescript --less
```

Now, let's start with the **Customers** page. Follow these steps to build the **Customers** page interface:

1. Add the `PageContainer` and the `ProTable` components to the `index.tsx` file under the `src/pages/Customer` folder as follows:

    ```
    import { PlusOutlined } from '@ant-design/icons';
    import { Button } from 'antd';
    import ProTable from '@ant-design/pro-table';
    import { FormattedMessage, getLocale } from 'umi';
    import { PageContainer } from '@ant-design/pro-layout';

    export default function Page() {
      return (
        <PageContainer style={{ minHeight: '90vh' }}>
          <ProTable<any>
            rowKey="id"
            headerTitle=
              {<FormattedMessage id="table.customer.title"
              />}
    ```

```
        search={{ labelWidth: 'auto' }}
        pagination={{ pageSize: 5 }}
        dateFormatter="string"
        locale={getLocale()}
        toolBarRender={() => [
          <Button key="button" icon={<PlusOutlined />}
            type="primary">
            <FormattedMessage id="table.new" />
          </Button>,
        ]}
      />
    </PageContainer>
  );
}
```

Notice that we use the FormattedMessage component to render the texts on this page, so we need to add these texts to multi-language files in the src/ locales folder.

2. Add the text present on the **Customers** page to the en-US.ts file as follows:

```
import menu from './en-US/menu';

export default {
  ...menu,

  'home.recents': 'Recent opportunities',
  'greetings.hello': 'Hello',
  'greetings.welcome': 'welcome',

  'table.opportunity.title': 'Opportunities',
  'table.customer.title': 'Customers',
};
```

3. Now, to access the **Customers** page, we need to define its route in the `routes.ts` file as follows:

```
{
    path: '/customers',
    name: 'customers',
    icon: 'user',
    component: '@/pages/Customers',
},
```

4. Add the customer menu item title to the `menu.ts` file under the `src/locales/en-US` folder as follows:

```
export default {
    'menu.opportunities': 'Opportunities',
    'menu.customers': 'Customers',
};
```

Now, let's build the **Opportunities** page following the steps demonstrated previously:

1. For the `headerTitle` property of `ProTable`, type the following:

```
headerTitle={<FormattedMessage id="table.opportunity.title" />}
```

2. Define the **Opportunities** page route as follows:

```
{
    path: '/opportunities',
    name: 'opportunities',
    icon: 'AccountBook',
    component: '@/pages/Opportunities',
},
```

3. Don't forget to add the texts to the `en-US.ts` and `menu.ts` files.

The result should look like this:

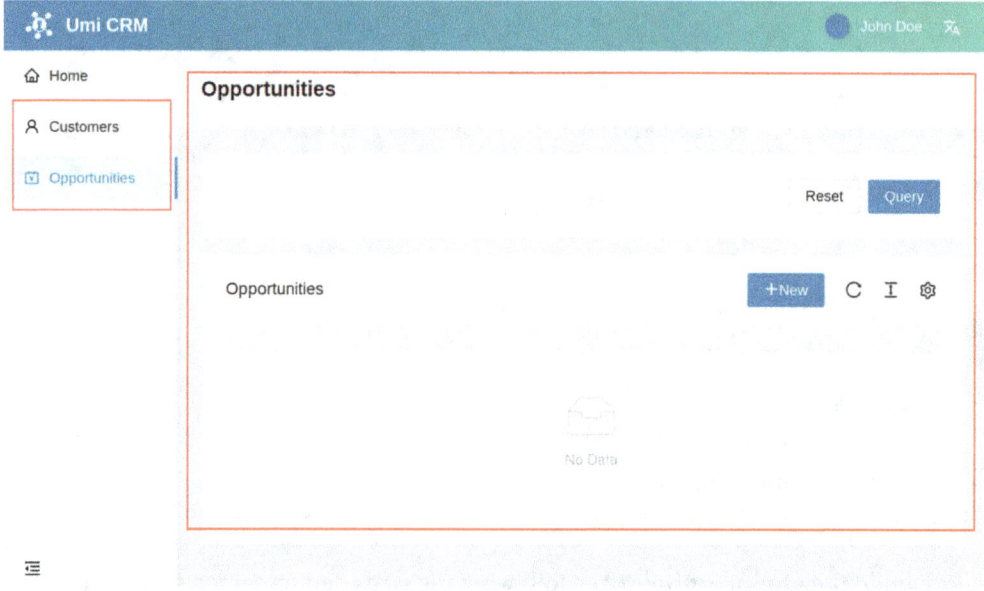

Figure 2.6 – Opportunities page layout and menu items

In this section, we created the **Opportunities** and **Customers** pages using the `ProTable` component with support for internationalization. Next, we'll build the **Reports** page.

Creating the Reports page

Now, we'll build the **Reports** page. Users can access helpful information on this page to get insights into the sales life cycle. We'll add three charts to this page using the chart component library bizcharts.

The bizcharts library is focused on business scenarios and dedicated to creating professional data visualization solutions. It's also an open source project licensed under the MIT license. You can learn more about bizcharts at `https://bizcharts.taobao.com/`:

1. First, run this command to install the bizcharts package:

    ```
    $ yarn add bizcharts
    ```

2. Next, run this command to generate the **Reports** page:

    ```
    $ yarn umi g page /Reports/index --typescript --less
    ```

Now, follow these steps to create the **Reports** page interface:

1. Let's define the page layout with `antd` components. Add the following components to the `index.tsx` file under the `src/pages/Reports` folder:

```
import { PageContainer } from '@ant-design/pro-layout';
import { Row, Col, Card } from 'antd';
import { FormattedMessage } from 'umi';
import {
  Chart,
  Coordinate,
  Axis,
  Legend,
  Interval,
  Tooltip,
  Interaction,
} from 'bizcharts';

const colProps = {
  style: { marginBottom: 24 },
  xs: 24,
  sm: 12,
  md: 12,
  lg: 12,
  xl: 12,
};

export default function Page() {
  return (
    <PageContainer>
      <Row gutter={24}>
        <Col {...colProps}></Col>
        <Col {...colProps}></Col>
      </Row>

      <Row gutter={24} style={{ padding: 10 }}></Row>
    </PageContainer>
```

```
    );
  }
```

We defined the layout with two responsive rows, and the first row has two responsive columns. The `colProps` variable sets how the columns should adjust their size at different breakpoints.

2. Now, let's add the first chart. This chart will show the four most important opportunities classified by the CRM analytics service. Add the `Chart` component from bizcharts inside the first column of the first row as follows:

```
<Card title={<FormattedMessage id="chart.top" />}>
  <Chart height={200} data={[]} autoFit>
    <Coordinate transpose />

    <Axis name="name" label={false} />
    <Axis
      name="revenue"
      label={{
        formatter: (text) => `$ ${text}`,
      }}
    />
    <Interval
      type="interval"
      label={["name", (name) => <>{name}</>]}
      tooltip={{
        fields: ["name", "revenue"],
        callback: (name, revenue) => {
          return { name: name, value: `$ ${revenue}` };
        },
      }}
      color={["name", "#3936FE-#14CCBE"]}
      position="name*revenue"
    />
    <Interaction type="element-single-selected" />
  </Chart>
</Card>
```

We can configure the `Chart` component with its children components. We set the chart to invert the *x* and *y* axis with the `Coordinate` component. With the `Axis` component, we defined a new axis called `revenue`. The `Interval` component described the chart type and the keys that will populate the axis using the `position` property.

Notice that we set an empty array in the `data` property. We'll put the information we want to display in the `data` property in the future.

3. Let's add the second chart. This chart will show where the customers come from and in what proportion. Add the `Chart` component to the second column of the first row as follows:

```
<Card title={<FormattedMessage id="chart.leads" />}>
  <Chart
    height={200}
    data={[]}
    scale={{
      percent: {
        formatter: (val: any) => {
          val = val * 100 + "%";
          return val;
        },
      },
    }}
    autoFit
  >
    <Coordinate type="theta" radius={0.95} />
    <Tooltip showTitle={false} />
    <Axis visible={false} />
    <Legend position="right" />
    <Interval
      position="percent"
      adjust="stack"
      color="source"
      style={{
        lineWidth: 1,
        stroke: "#fff",
```

```
      }}
    />
    <Interaction type="element-single-selected" />
  </Chart>
</Card>
```

In this chart, we set the `Coordinate` component to cylindrical coordinates to generate a pie chart. With the `Interaction` component, we set the chart to react when it is moused over or clicked.

4. The last chart shows the opportunities gained and lost by month. Add the `Chart` component to the second row as follows:

```
<Card
  style={{ width: '100%' }}
  title={<FormattedMessage id="chart.month" />}
>
  <Chart height={300} padding="auto" data={[]} autoFit>
    <Interval
      adjust={[
        {
          type: 'dodge',
          marginRatio: 0,
        },
      ]}
      color={['name', '#3776E7-#14CCBE']}
      position="month*value"
    />
    <Tooltip shared />
  </Chart>
</Card>
```

5. To finish the **Reports** page, let's add the following texts to the `en-US.ts` file under the `src/locales` folder:

```
'chart.top': 'Top opportunities',
'chart.leads': 'Leads by source',
'chart.month': 'Opportunities Won/Lost by month',
```

6. And add the following text to the `menu.ts` file under the `src/locales/en-US` folder:

```
'menu.reports': 'Reports',
```

7. Finally, configure the **Reports** page route in the `routes.ts` file as follows:

```
{
    path: '/reports',
    name: 'reports',
    icon: 'BarChartOutlined',
    component: '@/pages/Reports',
},
```

Now, the **Reports** page is finished and should look like this:

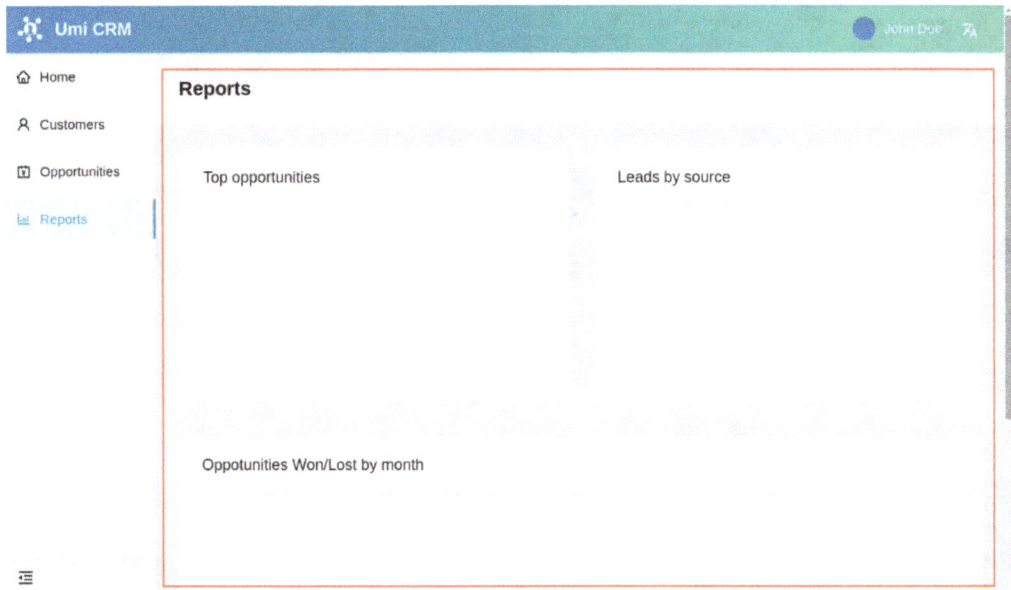

Figure 2.7 – Reports page layout

Notice that all chart cards are empty because we defined empty arrays in all chart `data` properties. We'll generate the data required to show the charts in the next chapter.

In this section, we created the **Reports** page using the bizcharts library. We added three charts to our page: a bar chart called **Top opportunities**, a pie chart called **Leads by source**, and a bar chart called **Opportunities Won/Lost by month**.

Summary

In this chapter, you were introduced to the project we'll build, the Ant Design React library, and Pro components. You also learned how to configure the layout using the UmiJS layout plugin and define and customize the global layout using the `global.less` file. You learned how to customize the application theme by changing the default LESS variables used by Ant Design components.

We also created and defined our application layout's right-side content to show the user's name, avatar, and a language selector. You learned how to set up internationalization using the UmiJS locale plugin and created the home page. Next, we made the **Customers** and **Opportunities** pages using the `ProTable` component.

Finally, we built the **Reports** page using **antd** library components to define the layout and the bizcharts library to render three charts.

In the next chapter, we'll generate a mock API, make requests to the backend, and learn how to use services and models.

3
Using Models, Services, and Mocking Data

One of the main features of a frontend web application is communication with the backend. Our application needs to collect user input and send it for processing.

In this chapter, you will learn how to define data by creating typescript interfaces and column definitions for the `ProTable` component. You will learn how to simulate the backend logic and data using Umi **mock files**. You will know how to send HTTP requests using the **umi-request** library. You will also learn to share states and logic between components using **models**.

We'll cover the following main topics:

- Defining response types and column types
- Creating the opportunity details page
- Simulating data and API responses
- Sending HTTP requests with Umi request
- Using models for sharing states and logic

By the end of this chapter, you'll have learned how the data flow works in Umi and how to organize your projects using the `services` and `models` folders. You'll also learn how to use the Umi features to simulate backend logic and send HTTP requests. You will also better understand how the `ProTable` component helps us to work with batches of data.

Technical requirements

To complete this chapter's exercises, you only need a computer with any OS (I recommend Ubuntu 20.04 or higher) and the software installed in *Chapter 1*, *Environment Setup and Introduction to UmiJS* (Visual Studio Code, Node.js, and Yarn).

You can find the complete project in the `Chapter03` folder in the GitHub repository available at `https://github.com/PacktPublishing/Enterprise-React-Development-with-UmiJs`.

Defining response types and column types

In this section, we will create TypeScript interfaces to define the data that we'll receive from the backend and create column definitions for the `ProTable` component on each page.

Let's start with the interfaces. Follow these steps to create the TypeScript interfaces:

1. Let's first create the folder for definition files. Under the `src` folder, create a new folder called `types`.

2. Now, in the `types` folder, create a new file named `user.d.ts` and add the following interface code:

```
export interface User {
  id?: number;
  name?: string;
  company?: string;
  role?: {
    id: number;
    title: string;
  };
  isLoggedIn: boolean;
}
```

The `User` interface defines how we'll receive user information from the backend.

3. Create a new file in the `types` folder named `customer.d.ts` and add the following interface:

```
export interface Customer {
    id?: number;
    name?: string;
    company?: string;
    phone?: string;
    email?: string;
    role?: string;
}
```

The `Customer` interface defines how we'll receive customer information from the backend.

4. Now, we'll create two interfaces for the `opportunity` model. Create a new file named `opportunity.d.ts` in the `types` folder and add the interfaces as follows:

```
import { Customer } from './customer';

export interface Opportunity {
    id: number;
    topic: string;
    budget: string;
    status: number;
    customer: Customer;
}

export interface Activity {
    id: number;
    type: number;
    schedule: Date;
    createdBy: string;
    summary: string;
}
```

The `Opportunity` interface defines how we'll receive the opportunity information from the backend.

Note that we imported the `Customer` interface and used it as the type of the `customer` property. An opportunity always relates to a specific customer registered in the CRM.

The `Activity` interface defines how we receive opportunities activity information from the backend.

5. Let's create the interfaces for the report's data. In the `types` folder, create a new file called `analytics.d.ts` and add the following interfaces:

```
export interface TopOpportunity {
  name: string;
  revenue: string;
}

export interface LeadsSource {
  source: string;
  count: number;
  percent: number;
}

export interface HistoryByMonth {
  name: string;
  month: string;
  value: string;
}
```

These interfaces define how we'll receive the data for the top opportunities chart, the leads by source chart, and the opportunities won/lost by month chart.

Now, let's define how the `ProTable` component on each page should display the data received from the backend.

Creating column definitions for ProTable

We need to set how the `ProTable` component will display data by defining the columns. I recommend you create column definitions in a separate file whenever possible to maintain the component code and keep it clean.

Follow these steps to create the column definitions on each page:

1. Let's start with the **Customers** page. Create a new file named `columns.tsx` in the `Customers` folder under the `src/pages` folder.

2. In the `columns.tsx` file, define the table columns as follows:

```tsx
import { Customer } from '@/types/customer';
import { ProColumns } from '@ant-design/pro-table';
import { FormattedMessage } from 'umi';


const columns: ProColumns<Customer>[] = [
  {
    title: <FormattedMessage id="table.customer.name"
          />,
    dataIndex: 'name',
  },
  {
    title: <FormattedMessage id="table.customer.email"
          />,
    dataIndex: 'email',
    copyable: true,
  },
  {
    title: <FormattedMessage id="table.customer.phone"
          />,
    dataIndex: 'phone',
  },
  {
    title: <FormattedMessage id="table.customer.role"
          />,
    dataIndex: 'role',
  },
  {
```

```
        title: <FormattedMessage
                id="table.customer.company" />,
        dataIndex: 'company',
    },
];
```

```
export default columns;
```

Note that we used the `Customer` interface to declare the data type. Each column definition has a `title` and a `dataIndex`. The latter needs to match a property of the `Customer` interface for `ProTable` to display that property value in its column.

3. Let's add a column to display options in a specific row. Add this definition to the `columns.tsx` file:

```
{
    title: <FormattedMessage id="table.options" />,
    valueType: 'option',
    hideInSetting: true,
    hideInDescriptions: true,
    render: (_, record, __, action) => [
      <a
        key="editable"
        onClick={() => {
          action?.startEditable(record.id as number);
        }}
      >
        <FormattedMessage id="table.edit" />
      </a>,
    ],
},
```

In the `options` column, besides the properties we set to not display the column in settings and descriptions, we set the behavior of the `render` function. This allows you to access the React node, the row entity, the index, and the default `ProTable` actions. When the user clicks on this option, the `startEditable` action allows them to edit the row.

4. Now, we'll use the column definitions in the `ProTable` component. Add the following line to the `index.tsx` file to import the `columns.tsx` file:

```
import columns from './columns';
```

5. Define the `ProTable` `columns` property with the imported file, as follows:

```
columns={columns}
```

6. Next, add the `Customer` interface to define the data type of the `ProTable` columns:

```
<ProTable<Customer>
```

7. Now, let's create the column definitions for the **Opportunities** page. Create a new file named `columns.tsx` in the `Opportunities` folder under the `src/pages` folder.

8. Add the definitions to the `columns.tsx` file, as follows:

```
import { Customer } from '@/types/customer';
import { Opportunity } from '@/types/opportunity';
import { ProColumns } from '@ant-design/pro-table';
import { Tag } from 'antd';
import { FormattedMessage, history } from 'umi';


const columns: ProColumns<Opportunity>[] = [
  {
    title: <FormattedMessage
             id="table.opportunity.topic" />,
    dataIndex: 'topic',
    width: 300,
  },
  {
    title: <FormattedMessage
             id="table.opportunity.budget" />,
    dataIndex: 'budget',
    render: (node) => <>{`$ ${node}`}</>,
  },
  {
    title: <FormattedMessage
             id="table.opportunity.status" />,
```

```
    dataIndex: 'status',
    valueType: 'select',
    hideInDescriptions: true,
    filters: true,
    onFilter: true,
  },
];

export default columns;
```

Note that we used the `Opportunity` interface we created previously to define the data type.

In the `status` column, we set the `valueType` property to `select`, and the `filters` and `onFilter` properties to `true`, so the user can choose and filter the table using this `column` value.

9. `status` is a numeric value representing the opportunity's progress in the sales flow. But, we want the user to see the title instead of a number, so let's add the `enumType` property to the `status` column, as follows:

```
valueEnum: {
  0: {
    text: (
      <Tag color="#8d79f2" key={0}>
        <FormattedMessage id="step.propose" />
      </Tag>
    ),
  },
  1: {
    text: (
      <Tag color="#c7f279" key={0}>
        <FormattedMessage id="step.develop" />
      </Tag>
    ),
  },
  2: {
    text: (
      <Tag color="#e379f2" key={0}>
```

```
            <FormattedMessage id="step.qualify" />
          </Tag>
      ),
    },
    3: {
      text: (
        <Tag color="#79f2e3" key={0}>
          <FormattedMessage id="step.close" />
        </Tag>
      ),
    },
  },
```

The status will appear as tags with different colors and the respective step title.

10. The opportunity relates to a customer, and we need to define columns for the customer properties. Let's add these columns as follows:

```
  {
    title: <FormattedMessage
          id="table.opportunity.customer" />,
    dataIndex: 'customer',
    render: (node) => <>{node && (node as
                              Customer).name}</>,
    editable: false,
  },
  {
    title: <FormattedMessage id="table.customer.email"
          />,
    dataIndex: 'customer',
    hideInTable: true,
    render: (node) => <>{node && (node as
                              Customer).email}</>,
    editable: false,
  },
  {
    title: <FormattedMessage id="table.customer.phone"
          />,
```

```
  dataIndex: 'customer',
  hideInTable: true,
  render: (node) => <>{node && (node as
                         Customer).phone}</>,
  editable: false,
},
{
  title: <FormattedMessage id="table.customer.company"
       />,
  dataIndex: 'customer',
  hideInTable: true,
  render: (node) => <>{node && (node as
                         Customer).company}</>,
  editable: false,
},
```

Note that the only column in the table is the customer's name. In the other columns, we set `hideInTable` to `true`. We'll use these columns in the opportunity details page that we'll create later in this chapter.

11. We'll also add a column to display options to a specific row in this table. Add this definition to the `columns.tsx` file:

```
{
  title: <FormattedMessage id="table.options" />,
  valueType: 'option',
  hideInSetting: true,
  hideInDescriptions: true,
  render: (_, record, __, action) => [
    <a
      key="editable"
      onClick={() => {
        action?.startEditable(record.id as number);
      }}
    >
      <FormattedMessage id="table.edit" />
    </a>,
    <a key="more" onClick={() =>
```

```
            history.push(`/opportunity/${record.id}`)}>
            <FormattedMessage id="table.more" />
        </a>,
    ],
},
```

The `options` column introduces two options – **Edit the row** and **Show more**. When users click for more, the umi history will redirect the user to the opportunity details page located in the `/opportunity/:id` path.

12. Now, we'll use the column definitions in the `ProTable` component. Add the following line to the `index.tsx` file to import the `columns.tsx` file:

```
import columns from './columns';
```

13. Define the `ProTable` `columns` property with the imported file, as follows:

```
columns={columns}
```

14. Import the `Opportunity` interface, as follows:

```
import { Opportunity } from '@/types/opportunity';
```

15. Next, add the `Opportunity` interface to define the data type of the `ProTable` columns:

```
<ProTable<Opportunity>
```

16. Follow these previous steps to add the column definitions to `ProTable` on the home page. We'll reuse the `columns.tsx` file from the **Opportunities** page, so you need to import the file, as follows:

```
import columns from '../Opportunities/columns';
```

17. Now, we need to add the texts to the multi-language files. Add the texts to the `en-US.ts` file in the `src/locales` folder, as follows:

```
'table.options': 'Options',
'table.edit': 'Edit',
'table.more': 'More',
'table.new': 'New',

'table.customer.title': 'Customers',
'table.customer.role': 'Role',
```

```
'table.customer.name': 'Name',
'table.customer.email': 'Email',
'table.customer.phone': 'Phone',
'table.customer.company': 'Company',
'form.customer.title': 'New customer',


'table.opportunity.assign': 'Assign Opportunities',
'table.opportunity.title': 'Opportunity',
'table.opportunity.detail': 'Details',
'table.opportunity.activities': 'Activities',
'table.opportunity.topic': 'Topic',
'table.opportunity.budget': 'Budget',
'table.opportunity.status': 'Step',
'table.opportunity.customer': 'Customer',
'form.opportunity.title': 'New opportunity',
```

We don't need to add these texts to the `pt-BR.ts` file because we already downloaded the complete file in the previous chapter.

In this section, we created the TypeScript interfaces to define all the data we'll receive from the backend and the column definitions for the `ProTable` component on each page.

Now, let's create the opportunity details page, which will show the activities on the opportunity.

Creating the opportunity details page

In this section, we'll create the opportunity details page. The opportunity details page allows the user to track and register opportunity activities.

The user can also change the opportunity step and edit the opportunity properties such as `title` and `expected revenue`.

Follow these steps to create the opportunity details page:

1. Run the following command to generate the opportunity detail page:

    ```
    yarn umi g page /OpportunityDetail/index --typeScript
    --less
    ```

2. We'll use a pro component called `ProDescriptions`. It's similar to the `ProTable` component but intended for display properties instead of a batch of data. Run the following command to add the `ProDescriptions` component to the project:

```
yarn add @ant-design/pro-descriptions@1.10.5
```

3. Next, import these dependencies to the `index.tsx` file in the `OpportunityDetail` folder, as follows:

```
import { Opportunity } from '@/types/opportunity';
import ProDescriptions from '@ant-design/
pro-descriptions';
import { Page Container } from '@ant-design/pro-layout';
import ProTable from '@ant-design/pro-table';
import { Breadcrumb, Button, Card, Steps, Tag } from
'antd';
import { useParams, history, FormattedMessage } from
'umi';
import columns from '../Opportunities/columns';
import { PlusOutlined } from '@ant-design/icons';
import { Activity } from '@/types/opportunity';
```

4. Now, create the `page` component in the `index.tsx` file, as follows:

```
export default function Page() {
  const { id } = useParams<{ id: string }>();

  return (
    <PageContainer
      extra={[
        <Button icon={<PlusOutlined />} key="activity"
          type="primary">
          <FormattedMessage id="activity.new" />
        </Button>,
      ]}
    >
      <Card bordered>
        <ProDescriptions<Opportunity>
          title={<FormattedMessage
```

```
                        id="table.opportunity.detail" />}
            columns={columns}
            dataSource={[]}
        />
    </Card>


    <Card bordered>
      <ProTable<Activity>
        headerTitle={<FormattedMessage
            id="table.opportunity.activities" />}
        rowKey="id"
        toolbar={{ settings: undefined }}
        search={false}
        pagination={{ pageSize: 5 }}
        columns={[]}
        params={{ customerId: id }}
        request={() => {}}
      />
    </Card>
  </PageContainer>
  );
}
```

Note that we accessed the ID we got from the route parameters. We will use it to request a specific opportunity from the backend.

We also used the ProDescriptions component to show the opportunity details and ProTable to list the opportunity activities.

5. The opportunity details page will only be accessible in the opportunities table row option and not accessible in the menu, so let's add a **breadcrumb** to help the user navigate thought the interfaces. Add the header property to the PageContainer component, as follows:

```
header={{
  title: <FormattedMessage
          id="table.opportunity.title" />,
  breadcrumb: (
    <Breadcrumb>
```

```
          <Breadcrumb.Item>
            <a onClick={() =>
              history.push('/opportunities')}>
              <FormattedMessage id="menu.opportunities" />
            </a>
          </Breadcrumb.Item>

          <Breadcrumb.Item>
            <FormattedMessage id="table.opportunity.title"
            />
          </Breadcrumb.Item>
        </Breadcrumb>
      ),
}}
```

6. Now, we'll add the `Steps` component from Ant Design to visually show the progress of the opportunity. Add the `Steps` component before the `ProDescriptions` component as the first child of the `Card` component, as follows:

```
<Steps current={0}>
  <Steps.Step
    key="quality"
    description={<Tag color="#e379f2" key={0} />}
    title={<FormattedMessage id="step.qualify" />}
  />

  <Steps.Step
    key="develop"
    description={<Tag color="#c7f279" key={1} />}
    title={<FormattedMessage id="step.develop" />}
  />

  <Steps.Step
    key="propose"
    description={<Tag color="#8d79f2" key={2} />}
    title={<FormattedMessage id="step.propose" />}
  />
```

```
<Steps.Step
  key="close"
  description={<Tag color="#42C3E3" key={3} />}
  title={<FormattedMessage id="step.close" />}
/>
</Steps>
<br />
```

The `current` property indicates the progress of the opportunity in the sales flow.

7. Now, add the route definition to the opportunity details page in the `routes.ts` file in the `config` folder, as follows:

```
{
  path: '/opportunity/:id',
  component: '@/pages/OpportunityDetail',
},
```

Note that we don't add the `name` and `icon` properties because we don't want the opportunity details page listed in the side menu.

We are almost finishing building the opportunity details page. Now, we'll use the `Activity` interface we created previously to define the columns of the activities table.

Defining the activities table columns

The opportunity details page lists the activities taken on the opportunity using the `ProTable` component, so we also need to define the columns for this table.

Follow these steps to define the columns for the `ProTable` component:

1. Create a new file named `columns.tsx` in the `OpportunityDetails` folder under the `src/pages` folder.

2. Next, add the column definitions to the `columns.tsx` file, as follows:

```
import { ProColumns } from '@ant-design/pro-table';
import { FormattedMessage } from 'umi';
import { Activity } from '@/types/opportunity';
import { Tag } from 'antd';

const columns: ProColumns<Activity>[] = [
```

```
    {
      title: <FormattedMessage
             id="table.activity.summary" />,
      dataIndex: 'summary',
      width: 300,
    },
    {
      title: <FormattedMessage id="table.activity.type"
             />,
      dataIndex: 'type',
    },
    {
      title: <FormattedMessage
             id="table.activity.schedule" />,
      valueType: 'date',
      dataIndex: 'schedule',
    },
    {
      title: <FormattedMessage
             id="table.activity.createdBy" />,
      dataIndex: 'createdBy',
    },
  ];

export default columns;
```

The type property is a numeric value representing the activity type.

3. We want the user to see a title instead of a numeric value in the type column, so let's add the enumType property to the type column, as follows:

```
valueEnum: {
  0: {
    text: (
      <Tag color="#42C3E3" key={0}>
        <FormattedMessage id="activity.call" />
      </Tag>
    ),
```

```
    },
    1: {
      text: (
        <Tag color="#42C3E3" key={1}>
          <FormattedMessage id="activity.email" />
        </Tag>
      ),
    },
    2: {
      text: (
        <Tag color="#42C3E3" key={2}>
          <FormattedMessage id="activity.meeting" />
        </Tag>
      ),
    },
    3: {
      text: (
        <Tag color="#42C3E3" key={3}>
          <FormattedMessage id="activity.event" />
        </Tag>
      ),
    },
  },
```

Now, the `type` column will show a tag with the activity type title in different colors.

4. Now, we'll use the column definitions in the `ProTable` component. Add the following line to the `index.tsx` file to import the `columns.tsx` file:

```
import activityColumns from './columns';
```

5. Next, define the `ProTable` `columns` property using the imported file, as follows:

```
columns={activityColumns}
```

6. To finish the opportunity details page, let's add the texts to the `en-US.ts` file in the `src/locales` folder, as follows:

```
'step.qualify': 'Qualify',
'step.develop': 'Develop',
```

```
'step.propose': 'Propose',
'step.close': 'Close',


'activity.call': 'Call',
'activity.email': 'Email',
'activity.meeting': 'Meeting',
'activity.event': 'Event',
'activity.new': 'New activity',


'table.activity.summary': 'Summary',
'table.activity.type': 'Type',
'table.activity.schedule': 'Scheduled',
'table.activity.createdBy': 'User',
```

In this section, we created the opportunity details page. We added a breadcrumb to help the user navigate between interfaces and the Steps component to show the opportunity progress. We also defined the activities table columns by creating the columns.tsx file.

Now, we are ready to learn how to simulate backend logic and API responses by creating Umi mock files.

Simulating data and API responses

In this section, you'll learn how to create mock files to simulate backend logic and API responses.

Mock files are helpful to decouple frontend development from backend development, as you don't need the backend ready to make requests and populate your interface with data.

A mock file is simply a JavaScript object with endpoint route definitions and a response to each endpoint. Consider the following example:

```
export default {
  'GET /api/products': { total: 0, products: [] },
};
```

In this example, when the project is running, we can send an HTTP GET request to http://localhost:8000/api/products to receive the object defined in the mock file.

Umi will registry all files with the .js and .ts extensions inside the mock folder as mock files.

Now that we know how mock files work, let's create mock files for our application. Follow these steps:

1. In the project root directory, create a new folder named mock.

2. Instead of manually generating the data we want to send, we'll use a library called **faker.js** to generate random data. The faker.js library delivers various data categories we can choose from, such as user profiles, company contacts, and product information. Run the following command to install the faker.js library:

    ```
    $ yarn add -D faker@5.5.3
    ```

3. Let's also add the TypeScript declaration files for faker.js by running the following command:

    ```
    $ yarn add -D @types/faker
    ```

4. Next, add the TypeScript declaration files for **express** by running the following command:

    ```
    $ yarn add -D @types/express
    ```

    We'll use the Response and Request interfaces from express to define the requests and responses in our mock endpoints.

5. Now, in the mock folder, create a new file named customer.ts.

6. In the customer.ts file, create a list of customers, as follows:

    ```
    import * as faker from 'faker';
    import { Response } from 'express';
    import { Customer } from '@/types/customer.d';

    const customers: Customer[] = [];

    for (let index = 0; index < 30; index++) {
      customers.push({
        id: index,
        name: faker.name.findName(),
        company: faker.company.companyName(),
        phone: faker.phone.phoneNumber(),
    ```

```
    role: faker.name.jobTitle(),
    email: faker.internet.email(),
  });
}
```

We used the `faker.js` library to generate random customer properties.

7. Next, create the endpoint route definitions in the `customer.ts` file, as follows:

```
export default {
  'PUT /api/customer': (_: any, res: Response) =>
    res.send({ success: true }),

  'PUT /api/customer/disable': (_: any, res: Response)
    =>
    res.send({ success: true }),

  '/api/customer/list': (_: any, res: Response) =>
    res.send({ data: customers, success: true }),

  'POST /api/customer': (_: any, res: Response) =>
    res.status(201).send({ success: true }),
};
```

We defined four endpoints:

- A mock endpoint to update the customer record (PUT /api/customer)
- A mock endpoint to disable the customer record (PUT /api/customer/disable)
- A mock endpoint to list all the customers (/api/customer/list)
- A mock endpoint to create a new customer record (POST /api/customer)

Note that we don't need to define the HTTP method when the endpoint uses the method GET as in the endpoint to list all customers (/api/customer/list).

8. Now, create a new file in the `mock` folder named `analytics.ts` and add the following:

```
import * as faker from 'faker';
import { Response } from 'express';


export default { }
```

We'll create data to populate the charts on the **Reports** page in this file.

9. In the `analytics.ts` file, create a new mock endpoint to deliver the top opportunities, as follows:

```
'/api/analytics/top/opportunity': (_: any, res: Response)
=>
    res.send({
      data: [
        { name: faker.commerce.productName(),
          revenue: 15000 },
        { name: faker.commerce.productName(),
          revenue: 30000 },
        { name: faker.commerce.productName(),
          revenue: 40000 },
        { name: faker.commerce.productName(),
          revenue: 50000 },
      ],
      success: true,
    }),
```

10. Next, create a mock endpoint to deliver the leads by source, as follows:

```
'/api/analytics/leads/source': (_: any, res: Response) =>
    res.send({
      data: [
        { source: 'Social Media', count: 40,
          percent: 0.4 },
        { source: 'Email Marketing', count: 21,
          percent: 0.21 },
        { source: 'Campaigns', count: 17,
          percent: 0.17 },
```

```
        { source: 'Landing Page', count: 13,
          percent: 0.13 },
        { source: 'Events', count: 9, percent: 0.09 },
      ],
    success: true,
  }),
```

11. Finally, create a mock endpoint to deliver the opportunities won/lost by month, as follows:

```
'/api/analytics/bymonth/opportunity': (_: any, res:
Response) =>
    res.send({
      data: [
        { name: 'Won', month: 'Jan.', value: 18 },
        { name: 'Won', month: 'Feb.', value: 28 },
        { name: 'Won', month: 'Mar.', value: 39 },
        { name: 'Won', month: 'Apr.', value: 81 },
        { name: 'Won', month: 'May', value: 47 },
        { name: 'Won', month: 'Jun.', value: 20 },
        { name: 'Won', month: 'Jul.', value: 24 },
        { name: 'Won', month: 'Aug.', value: 35 },
        { name: 'Lost', month: 'Jan.', value: 12 },
        { name: 'Lost', month: 'Feb.', value: 23 },
        { name: 'Lost', month: 'Mar.', value: 34 },
        { name: 'Lost', month: 'Apr.', value: 99 },
        { name: 'Lost', month: 'May', value: 52 },
        { name: 'Lost', month: 'Jun.', value: 35 },
        { name: 'Lost', month: 'Jul.', value: 37 },
        { name: 'Lost', month: 'Aug.', value: 42 },
      ],
    success: true,
  }),
```

12. Now, we'll create a mock file for the opportunities. Create a new file in the `mock` folder called `opportunity.ts` and add the following:

```ts
import * as faker from 'faker';
import { Opportunity, Activity } from '@/types/
opportunity.d';
import { Request, Response } from 'express';

const opportunity: Opportunity[] = [];
const activities: Activity[] = [];

for (let index = 0; index < 5; index++) {
  activities.push({
    id: index,
    type: faker.datatype.number({ max: 3, min: 0,
      precision: 1 }),
    schedule: faker.date.recent(),
    createdBy: faker.name.findName(),
    summary: faker.lorem.words(6),
  });
}

for (let index = 0; index < 30; index++) {
  opportunity.push({
    id: index,
    topic: faker.commerce.productName(),
    customer: {
      id: index,
      name: faker.name.findName(),
      company: faker.company.companyName(),
      phone: faker.phone.phoneNumber(),
      role: faker.name.jobTitle(),
      email: faker.internet.email(),
    },
    budget: faker.finance.amount(100000),
    status: faker.datatype.number({ max: 3, min: 0,
      precision: 1 }),
```

```
  });
}
```

We created two lists, `activities` and `opportunities`, and used the `faker.` `js` library to fill these lists with random data.

13. Next, create these two methods:

```
const listOpportunities = (req: Request, res: Response)
=> {
  const { slice } = req.query;

  res.send({
    data: opportunity.slice(0, slice ? Number(slice) :
      undefined),
    success: true,
  });
};

const getOpportunity = (req: Request, res: Response) => {
  const { opportunityId } = req.query;

  res.send(opportunity[Number(opportunityId)]);
};
```

The `listOpportunities` method slices the `opportunities` array using the number given in the `slice` request query parameter.

The `getOpportunity` method accesses the `opportunity` array item at the index position provided by the `opportunityId` request query parameter.

14. Finally, create the definitions of the mock endpoints, as follows:

```
export default {
  '/api/opportunity/list': listOpportunities,

  '/api/opportunity': getOpportunity,

  '/api/opportunity/activities': (_: any, res:
    Response) =>
    res.send({ data: activities, success: true }),
```

```
    'POST /api/opportunity': (_: any, res: Response) =>
        res.status(201).send({ success: true }),

    'PUT /api/opportunity/disable': (_: any, res:
        Response) =>
        res.send({ success: true }),

    'PUT /api/opportunity': (_: any, res: Response) =>
        res.send({ success: true }),
};
```

We defined six endpoints:

- A mock endpoint to list all the opportunities (/api/opportunity/list)
- A mock endpoint to get an opportunity by ID (/api/opportunity)
- A mock endpoint to get opportunity activities (/api/opportunity/activities)
- A mock endpoint to create a new opportunity record (POST /api/opportunity)
- A mock endpoint to disable an opportunity record (PUT /api/opportunity/disable)
- A mock endpoint to update an opportunity record (PUT /api/opportunity)

In this section, we created mock files to provide data for our interfaces using the faker.js library to generate random data.

Now, we'll learn how to organize our project with the services folder and send requests to our simulated backend using the umi-request library.

Sending HTTP requests with Umi request

In this section, we'll develop the requests to the backend using the umi-request library.

We'll create all the requests in separate files inside the services folder for each context. This organization helps us clean the components' code and reuses the requests over the interfaces.

For sending HTTP requests, we'll use **Umi request**. This is a library based in the **fetch** and **axios** libraries that is simple to use and provides common features such as error handling and caching. Consider the following example:

```
request<Product>('/api/products', {
  method: 'POST',
  headers: { Authorization: 'Bearer eyJhbGciOi...' },
  params: { onSale: true },
  data: {
    id: 0,
    title: 'My product',
    price: 10.0,
  },
});
```

The `request` function requires two main parameters – the `URL` parameter where we want to send the request, and the `options` parameter in which we can define the HTTP method, the request headers, the request parameters, and the request body in the `data` property. You can also determine the response type. In this example, we described the response type with the `Product` interface.

Follow these steps to develop the requests:

1. Create a new folder named `services` in the `src` folder.

2. Inside the `services` folder, create a new file named `analytics.ts` and the requests, as follows:

```
import { HistoryByMonth, LeadsSource, TopOpportunity, }
from '@/types/analytics';
import { request } from 'umi';

export function getTopOpportunities() {
  return request<{ data: TopOpportunity[];
    success: boolean }>(
    `/api/analytics/top/opportunity`,
    {
      method: 'GET',
    },
  );
```

```
}

export function getLeadsBySource() {
  return request<{ data: LeadsSource[];
    success: boolean }>(
    `/api/analytics/leads/source`,
    {
      method: 'GET',
    },
  );
}

export function getHistoryByMonth() {
  return request<{ data: HistoryByMonth[];
    success: boolean }>(
    `/api/analytics/bymonth/opportunity`,
    {
      method: 'GET',
    },
  );
}
```

We created three functions – `getTopOpportunities` to request the top opportunities, `getLeadsBySource` to request the leads by source, and `getHistoryByMonth` to request the opportunities won/lost by month.

3. Now, we can use the requests response to fill our charts data source on the **Reports** page. Add the following to the `index.tsx` file in the `pages/Reports` folder:

```
const [leadsBySource, setLeadsBySource] =
  useState<LeadsSource[]>([]);
const [historyByMonth, setHistoryByMonth] =
  useState<any[]>([]);
const [topOpp, setTopOpp] =
  useState<TopOpportunity[]>([]);

useEffect(() => {
  const fetchTopOpp = async () => {
```

```
        setTopOpp((await getTopOpportunities()).data);
    };

    const fetchLeadsBySource = async () => {
        setLeadsBySource((await getLeadsBySource()).data);
    };

    const fetchHistoryByMonth = async () => {
        setHistoryByMonth((await
                            getHistoryByMonth()).data);
    };

    fetchHistoryByMonth();
    fetchLeadsBySource();
    fetchTopOpp();
}, []);
```

We created three states using the `useState` React hook to store our charts data and utilized the `useEffect` React hook to fill our charts with data when the page is rendered.

4. Import all the React dependencies and functions from the `analytics.ts` file, as follows:

```
import { useState, useEffect } from 'react';
import {
    getHistoryByMonth,
    getLeadsBySource,
    getTopOpportunities,
} from '@/services/analytics';
```

5. Next, add each state to the data property of the corresponding Chart component. The result should look like the following:

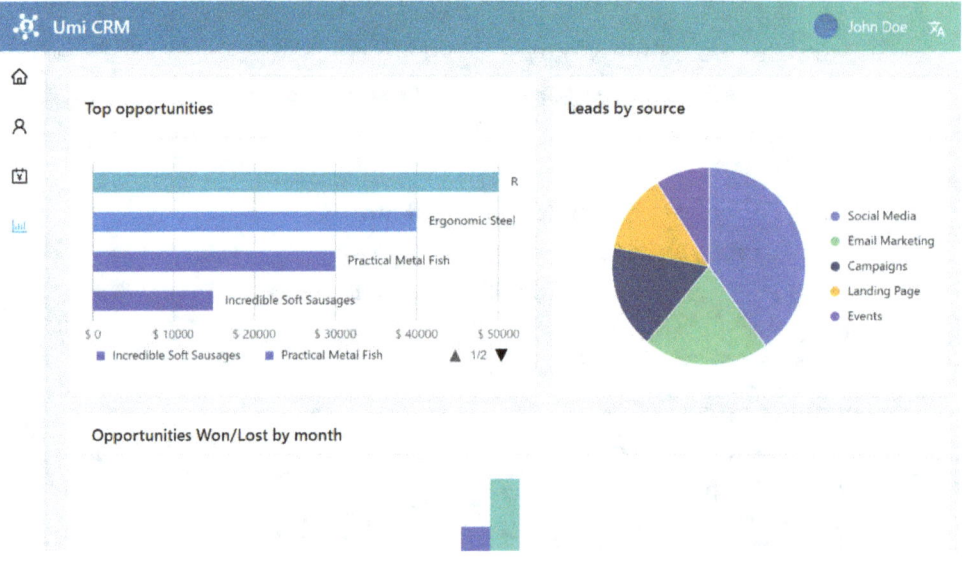

Figure 3.1 – The Reports page charts filled with data

6. Let's create the requests for the customer page. In the services folder, create a new file named customer.ts and write the requests, as follows:

```
import { Customer } from '@/types/customer';
import { request } from 'umi';


export function listCustomers(params?: any) {
  return request<{ data: Customer[]; success: boolean
    }>(`/api/customer/list`, {
    method: 'GET',
    params,
  });
}


export function createCustomer(customer: Customer) {
  return request<{ success: boolean
    }>(`/api/customer`, {
    method: 'POST',
    data: customer,
```

```
    });
}

export function disableCustomer(customerId?: string) {
    return request<{ success: boolean
      }>(`/api/customer/disable`, {
      method: 'PUT',
      params: { customerId },
    });
}

export function updateCustomer(customer: Customer) {
    return request<{ success: boolean
      }>(`/api/customer`, {
      method: 'PUT',
      data: customer,
    });
}
```

We created four functions – listCustomers to list all the customers, createCustomer to post a new customer record, disableCustomer to disable a customer record, and updateCustomer to update a customer record.

7. Now, we can list a customer in the ProTable component on the customer page. Import the listCustomers function to the index.tsx file in the pages/ Customers folder by adding the following line:

```
import { listCustomers } from '@/services/customer';
```

8. Next, add the listCustomers function to the request property of the ProTable component, as follows:

```
request={listCustomers}
```

The result should look like the following:

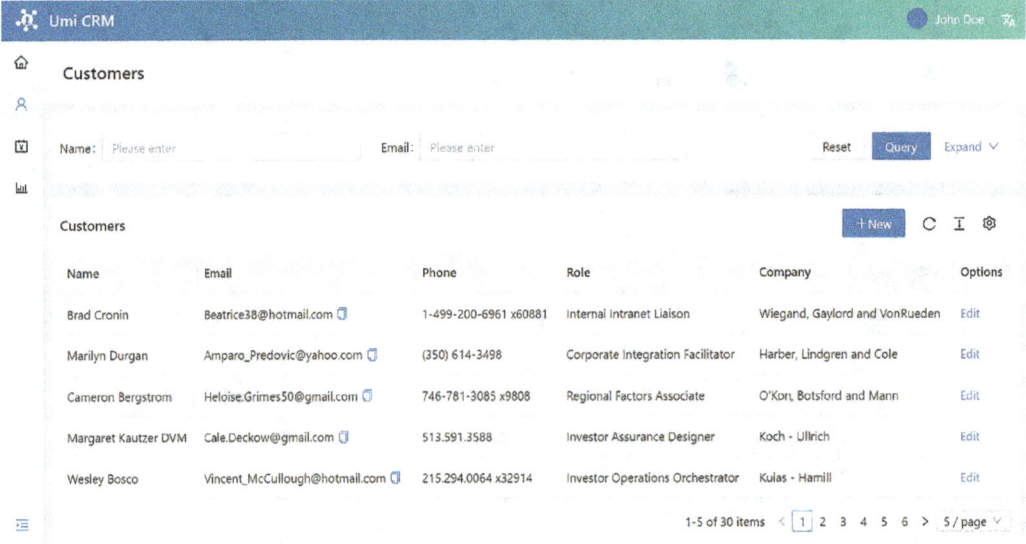

Figure 3.2 – The Customers list in the ProTable component

9. Finally, we'll create the requests on the opportunity page. Create a new file named `opportunity.ts` in the `services` folder.

10. Create the following functions in the `opportunity.ts` file, as follows:

```
import { Opportunity, Activity } from '@/types/
opportunity';
import { request } from 'umi';


export function listOpportunities(params?: any) {
  return request<{ data: Opportunity[];
    success: boolean }>(
    `/api/opportunity/list`,
    {
      method: 'GET',
      params,
    },
  );
}


export function listActivities(params?: any) {
```

```
  return request<{ data: Activity[];
    success: boolean }>(
    `/api/opportunity/activities`,
    {
      method: 'GET',
      params,
    },
  );
}

export function getOpportunity(params?: any) {
  return request<Opportunity>(`/api/opportunity`, {
    method: 'GET',
    params,
  });
}
```

We created three functions – listOpportunities to get all the opportunities, listActivities to list all the opportunity activities, and getOpportunity to get an opportunity by ID.

11. Next, create the other three functions in the opportunity.ts file, as follows:

```
export function createOpportunity(opportunity:
Opportunity) {
  return request<{ success: boolean
    }>(`/api/opportunity`, {
    method: 'POST',
    data: opportunity,
  });
}

export function disableOpportunity(opportunityId?:
string) {
  return request<{ success: boolean
    }>(`/api/opportunity/disable`, {
    method: 'PUT',
    params: { opportunityId },
```

```
    });
}

export function updateOpportunity(opportunity:
Opportunity) {
    return request<{ success: boolean
        }>(`/api/opportunity`, {
        method: 'PUT',
        data: opportunity,
    });
}
```

We created three more functions – createOpportunity to create a new opportunity record, disableOpportunity to disable an opportunity record, and updateOpportunity to update an opportunity record.

12. Now, we can list an opportunity in the ProTable component on the opportunity page. Add the following import to the index.tsx file in the pages/ Opportunity folder:

```
import { listOpportunities } from '@/services/
opportunity';
```

13. Next, add the listOpportunities function to the request property of the ProTable component, as follows:

```
request={listOpportunities}
```

The result should look like the following:

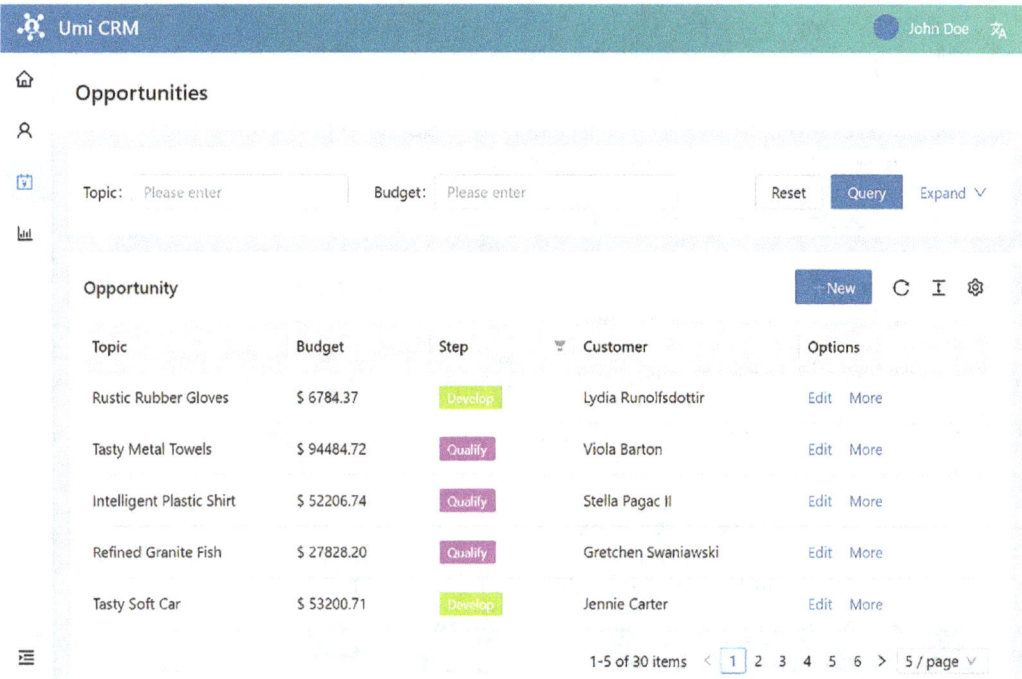

Figure 3.3 – The Opportunity list on the ProTable component

14. Let's also get the opportunity and list the opportunity activities on the opportunity details page. Import the following to the opportunity details page:

```
import { useEffect, useState } from 'react';
import { getOpportunity, listActivities } from '@/
services/opportunity';
```

15. Next, add the state to store the opportunity and the effect to request it, as follows:

```
const [opportunity, setOpportunity] =
  useState<Opportunity>();


useEffect(() => {
  const fetchOpportunity = async () => {
    setOpportunity(await getOpportunity({
      opportunityId: id }));
  };
```

```
    fetchOpportunity();
}, [])
```

16. Next, add the `opportunity` state to the `dataSource` property of the `ProDescriptions` component, as follows:

```
dataSource={opportunity}
```

17. Let's also add the `listActivities` function to the `request` property of the `ProTable` components, as follows:

```
request={listActivities}
```

18. Add the `opportunity status` property to the `current` property of the `Step` component, as follows:

```
current={opportunity?.status}
```

Now, the opportunity details page should look like the following:

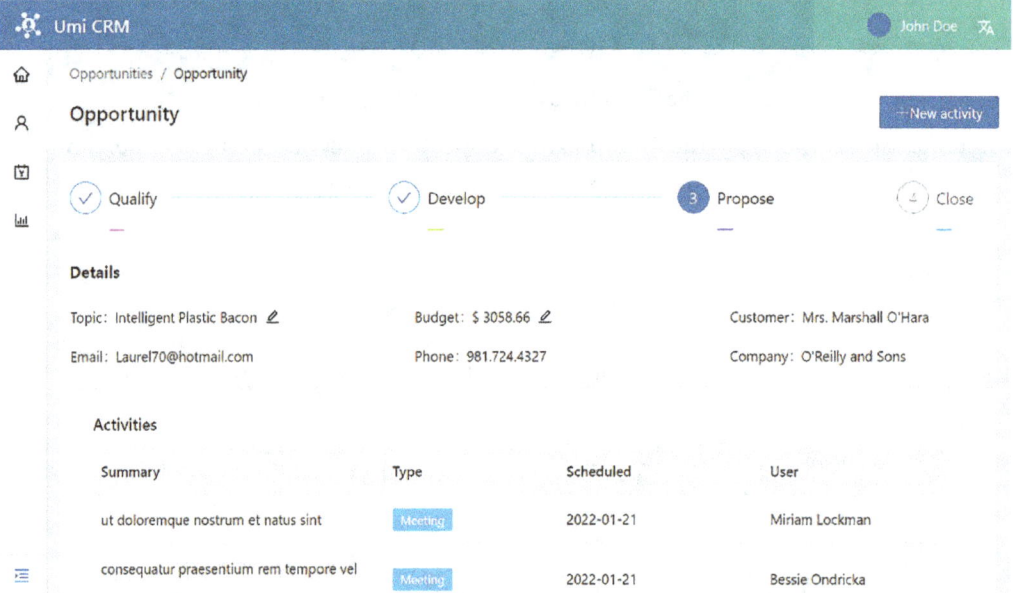

Figure 3.4 – Opportunity – Details and the Activities list

In this section, we created the `services` folder and the request for each page using the umi-request library. We also used the request on each page to access the data to fill our interfaces. Next, we'll learn to share states and logic between components by creating model files.

Using models for sharing states and logic

In this section, we'll create models for sharing states and logic between components.

A model is a special custom React hook to centralize the states and logic for a specific context.

We must create the models' files inside the `src/models` folder, and we can access these models using the `useModel` custom hook, as follows:

```
const { currentUser } = useModel('user');
```

Here, the `user` namespace matches the model filename, so the model file must be named `user.ts`.

Let's create the `customer` model and the `opportunity` model to demonstrate the use of models. These two models will contain the logic and result for creating, reading, and updating operations and share these operations between different interfaces.

Follow these steps to create the models:

1. Create a new folder called `models` inside the `src` folder.

2. Next, create a new file named `customer.ts` under the `models` folder and add the following:

```typescript
import { useCallback, useState } from 'react';
import { Customer } from '@/types/customer';
import {
  disableCustomer,
  updateCustomer,
  createCustomer,
} from '@/services/customer';

export interface CustomerModel {
  disable: (customerId: string) => void;
  update: (customer: Customer) => void;
  create: (customer: Customer) => void;
  clearResult: () => void;
  result: { success?: boolean };
}
```

We created the `CustomerModel` interface to describe all the functions and states we want to share between components.

3. Now, create the functions and state, as follows:

```
export default (): CustomerModel => {
  const [result, setResult] = useState<{
    success?: boolean }>({
    success: false,
  });

  const disable = useCallback(async (
    customerId?: string) => {
    setResult(await disableCustomer(customerId));
  }, []);

  const update = useCallback(async (
    customer: Customer) => {
    setResult(await updateCustomer(customer));
  }, []);

  const create = useCallback(async (
    customer: Customer) => {
    setResult(await createCustomer(customer));
  }, []);

  const clearResult = useCallback(() => setResult({
    success: false }), []);

  return { disable, update, create, clearResult,
    result };
};
```

We created a state to store the result and used the requests from the `services` files to execute the operations.

4. Let's use the `customer` model functions in the `ProTable` component on the **Customers** page. Add the following to the `index.tsx` file in the `pages/Customer` folder:

```
const { disable, update, clearResult, result } =
  useModel('customer');

const { formatMessage } = useIntl();

useEffect(() => {
  if (result?.success) {
    message.success(formatMessage({
      id: 'messages.success.operation' }));

    clearResult();
  }
}, [result]);
```

We used the `result` state to determine whether the operation succeeded and showed a success message.

5. Add the `editable` property to the `ProTable` component using the `model` functions, as follows:

```
editable={{
  type: 'multiple',
  deletePopconfirmMessage: <FormattedMessage
    id="table.confirm" />,
  deleteText: <FormattedMessage id="table.disable" />,
  onDelete: async (key) => disable(key as string),
  onSave: async (_, record) => update(record),
}}
```

We used the `disable` and `update` functions to provide the editable feature in the `ProTable` component.

6. Now, repeat the previous steps to create the `opportunity` model and enable the editable feature in the **Opportunities** page's `ProTable` component.

7. Add the text to the `en-US.ts` file under the `locales` folder, as follows:

```
'table.disable': 'Disable',
'table.confirm': 'Do you want to disable the record?',
```

Now, you can edit the records on both pages, as shown in the following screenshot:

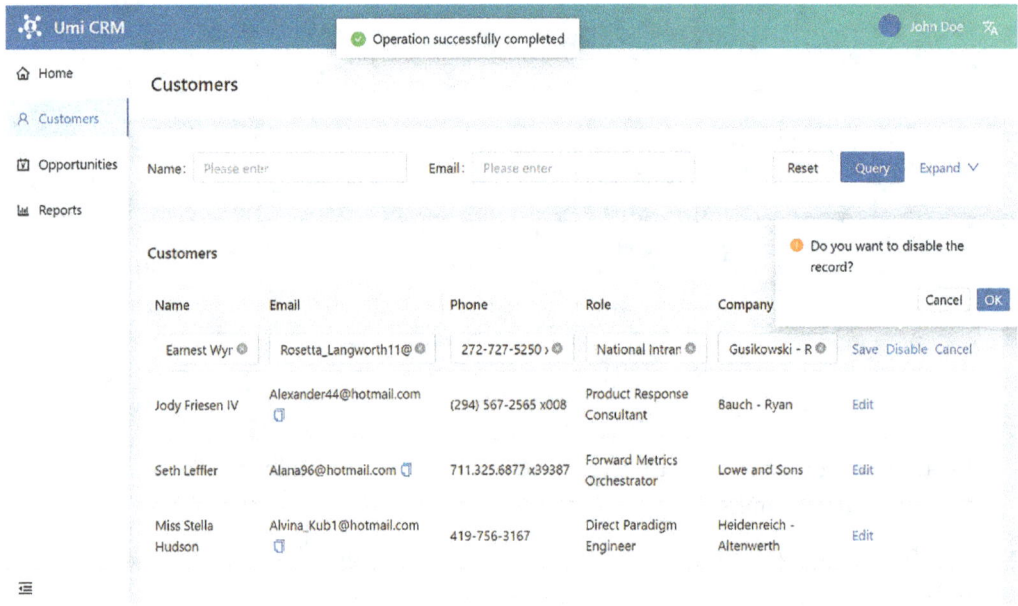

Feature 3.5 – The ProTable editable feature on the Customers page

In this section, you learned how models work. We created the `customer` and `opportunity` models for sharing states and logic and used them in the **Customers** and **Opportunities** pages to enable the `ProTable` editable feature.

Summary

In this chapter, we created the definition files for all the backend data and created the `ProTable` column definitions on each page. We created the opportunity details page using the `ProDescritions` component and the `Activity` interface to describe the opportunity activities.

You learned how Umi mock files work and how to create mock endpoints to provide simulated backend data and logic by creating the mock files for our application. Next, you learned how to organize your application requests using the `services` folder and send requests using the umi-request library by creating the `services` files for our application. Finally, you learned how models work and created the `customer` and `opportunity` models to share logic and state between components.

In the next chapter, you will learn how to handle API error responses by configuring the umi-request library, protecting routes using **plugin-access**, and storing and globally accessing user information after login.

Part 2: Protecting, Testing, and Deploying Web Applications

This section aims to teach the readers how to build a high-quality application by implementing software tests and clean code style and finally how to deploy it to online services. The reader will learn to handle errors, protect routes, learn to configure and use formattings tools, understand and write software tests and host the application on AWS.

This section comprises the following chapters:

- *Chapter 4, Error Handling, Authentication, and Route Protection*
- *Chapter 5, Code Style and Formatting Tools*
- *Chapter 6, Testing Front-End Applications*
- *Chapter 7, Single-Page Application Deployment*

4

Error Handling, Authentication, and Route Protection

We need to implement error handling and security measures in our interfaces to ensure that the quality and user experience of the application is good.

In this chapter, we'll modify the login page created in *Chapter 1*, *Environment Setup and Introduction to UmiJS* and configure the default HTML template for our application. You'll learn how to store and globally access data by configuring your application's initial state. Next, you'll learn how to block unauthorized access using the Umi `plugin-access`. Finally, you'll learn how to handle HTTP error responses and display feedback messages by configuring Umi requests.

In this chapter, we'll cover the following main topics:

- Modifying the login page and defining the HTML template
- Storing and globally accessing user information
- Protecting application routes based on user roles
- Handling HTTP error responses

By the end of this chapter, you'll have learned how to configure and use `plugin-initial-state` to store and access information globally in your application. You'll also have learned how to configure and use `plugin-access` to protect routes. Finally, you'll have learned how to handle HTTP error responses by configuring the umi-request library.

Technical requirements

To complete this chapter's exercises, you only need a computer with any OS (I recommend Ubuntu 20.04 or higher) and the software installed in *Chapter 1*, *Environment Setup and Introduction to UmiJS* (VS Code, Node.js, and Yarn).

You can find the complete project of this chapter in the `Chapter04` folder in the GitHub repository available at `https://github.com/PacktPublishing/Enterprise-React-Development-with-UmiJs`.

Modifying the login page and defining the HTML template

In this section, we'll create a Umi mock file and requests to simulate user authentication, a login page for users to log in, and we'll configure the default HTML template for our application.

Let's start with the mock file. We'll create endpoints for login, logout, and getting user information. Follow these steps to create the file:

1. Create a new file named `user.ts` in the `mock` folder. Next, create the `login` function as follows:

    ```
    import { User } from '@/types/user.d';
    import { Request, Response } from 'express';

    const user: { currentUser: User } = {
      currentUser: {
        isLoggedIn: false,
      },
    };
    ```

```
const login = (req: Request, res: Response) => {
  const { email, password } = req.body;
};
```

2. Add the following `if` statement to the `login` function:

```
if (email == 'john@doe.com' && password == 'user') {
  user.currentUser = {
    id: 0,
    name: 'John Doe',
    company: 'Umi Group',
    role: {
      id: 1,
      title: 'Inside Sales',
    },
    isLoggedIn: true,
  };

  res.json(user.currentUser);
}
```

Here, we defined a condition that allows the mock user John Doe, the inside sales representative, to access the application. The user role will determine what actions the user can execute and which pages they can access.

3. Next, add the following `else if` and `else` statements to the `login` function:

```
else if (email == 'marry@doe.com' &&
         password == 'admin') {
  user.currentUser = {
    id: 1,
    name: 'Marry Doe',
    company: 'Umi Group',
    role: {
      id: 0,
      title: 'Sales Manager',
    },
    isLoggedIn: true,
  };
```

```
      res.json(user.currentUser);
    } else {
      res.status(401).send();
    }
```

Here, we defined a condition that allows the mock user Mary Doe, the sales manager, to access the application. We also determined that if the user is not John Doe or Marry Doe, the mock API will return an HTTP 401 error, the status code for not authenticated.

4. Finally, add the other functions and the endpoint route definitions to the user.ts file as follows:

```
const logout = (_: any, res: Response) => {
  user.currentUser = { isLoggedIn: false };
  res.send({ success: true });
};


const getUser = (_: any, res: Response) => {
  if (!user.currentUser.isLoggedIn) {
    res.status(204).send();
  } else {
    res.json(user.currentUser);
  }
};


export default {
  'POST /api/login': login,
  'POST /api/logout': logout,
  '/api/currentUser': getUser,
};
```

We created the functions to simulate logout and get the logged-in user's information.

Now, we need to create requests in the `services` folder to get user info, login, and log out of the application. Follow these steps to create the requests:

1. Create a new file named `user.ts` in the `services` folder under the `src` folder.

2. Add the following requests to the `user.ts` file:

```
import { User } from '@/types/user.d';
import { request } from 'umi';

export function getCurrentUser() {
  return request<User>(`/api/currentUser`, {
    method: 'GET',
  });
}

export function userLogin(email: string,
  password: string) {
  return request<User>(`/api/login`, {
    method: 'POST',
    headers: { 'Content-Type': 'application/json' },
    data: { email, password },
  });
}

export function userLogout() {
  return request<void>(`/api/logout`, {
    method: 'POST',
  });
}
```

We created the requests to access the endpoints defined in the `user.ts` mock file.

We created a Umi mock file for simulating the user service and the requests to the backend. Now, we'll create a login page for users to input their email and password and authenticate in the application.

Modifying the login page

We need a login page for users to log in using their email and password. We have already created a login page using Umi UI in *Chapter 1*, *Environment Setup and Introduction to UmiJS*, so we only need to adapt the page components. Follow these steps to adjust the login page to match our theme:

1. Refactor the `index.tsx` file in the `pages/Login` folder as follows:

```tsx
import { SelectLang, useModel, history } from 'umi';
import styles from './index.less';
import LoginForm from './LoginForm';

export default function Page() {
  return (
    <div>
      <span className={styles.header}>
        <span className={styles.logo}>
          <img
            height={45}
            alt="crm logo"
            src="https://img.icons8.com/ios-filled/
              50/ffffff/customer-insight.png"
          />
             
          <h1 className={styles.title}>Umi CRM</h1>
        </span>
        <SelectLang className={styles.language} />
      </span>

      <div className={styles.container}>
        <LoginForm />
      </div>
    </div>
  );
}
```

We created a page header to display our application's logo and the language selector.

2. Now, add the CSS classes to style the title, the language selector, and the login form container in the `index.less` file as follows:

```less
@import '~antd/es/style/themes/default.less';

.title {
  text-align: center;
}

.container {
  display: flex;
  flex-direction: column;
  align-items: center;
}

.language {
  color: white;
}
```

3. Next, add the CSS class to style the header and logo in the `index.less` file as follows:

```less
.header {
  display: flex;
  flex-flow: row nowrap;
  justify-content: space-between;
  padding: 10px;
  margin-bottom: 20px;
  background: #1895bb;
  background: linear-gradient(50deg, #1895bb 0%,
                             #14cfbd 100%);

  > .logo {
    width: 95%;
    display: flex;
    flex-flow: row nowrap;
    justify-content: center;
    > h1 {
```

```
        color: white;
      }
    }
  }
```

4. Let's also make some changes to the `LoginForm` component styles. Refactor the `index.less` file in the `LoginForm` folder as follows:

```
@import '~antd/es/style/themes/default.less';

.container {
  :global {
    #components-form-demo-normal-login .login-form {
      width: 450px;
      margin: 5%;

      @media screen and (max-width: @screen-sm) {
        width: 90%;
      }
    }
    #components-form-demo-normal-login
      .login-form-forgot {
      float: right;
    }
    #components-form-demo-normal-login
      .login-form-button {
      width: 100%;
    }
  }
}
```

We modified the form's `width` and `margin` and defined `width` as `100%` on small screens using the `@screen-sm` breakpoint from the default Ant Design variables.

These are all the changes we need on the login page. The result should look like the following:

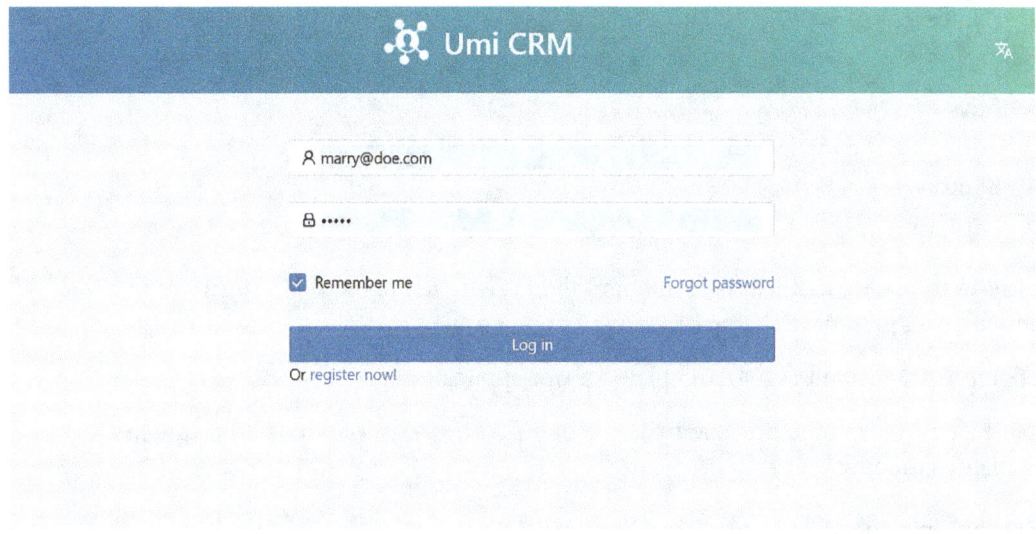

Figure 4.1 – Login page with the theme applied

If you access our application on a mobile device, you will notice that it doesn't seem right, although we have developed a fully responsive login page. We'll learn how to solve this problem by defining the application's default template.

Defining the default HTML template

If you are familiar with developing responsive websites, you'll know that the problem with our application pages is the **viewport** scale on mobile devices. We need to provide an HTML meta tag with the correct viewport attributes on each application page to solve the problem. As you already know, our application is a **single-page application** (**SPA**), so we only need to modify one HTML document.

Umi provides an option to customize the default HTML template for our application, which is the `document.ejs` file. If a file named `document.ejs` exists in the `src/pages` folder, Umi will use it as the default HTML document.

You can also access the application configuration in the `document.ejs` file using the `context.config` variable. Consider the following example:

```
<!doctype html>
<html>
<head>
  <title>
    <%= context.config.layout.title %>
```

```
    </title>
  </head>
  <body>
    <div id="root"></div>
  </body>
</html>
```

In this example, we defined the content of the HTML title tag as the `layout.title` configuration present in the `config/config.ts` file.

Let's create the default HTML template for our application.

Create a new file named `document.ejs` in the `src/pages` folder, and create the template as follows:

```
<!doctype html>
<html>

<head>
  <meta charset="utf-8" />
  <meta name="viewport" content="width=device-width,
    initial-scale=1.0" />
  <title>Umi CRM</title>
</head>

<body style="background-color: whitesmoke;">
  <div id="root"></div>
</body>

</html>
```

We set the viewport scale to `1.0` and the content width to the same device screen width.

The following screenshot shows the difference between the login page with the viewport meta tag on a mobile device and without it:

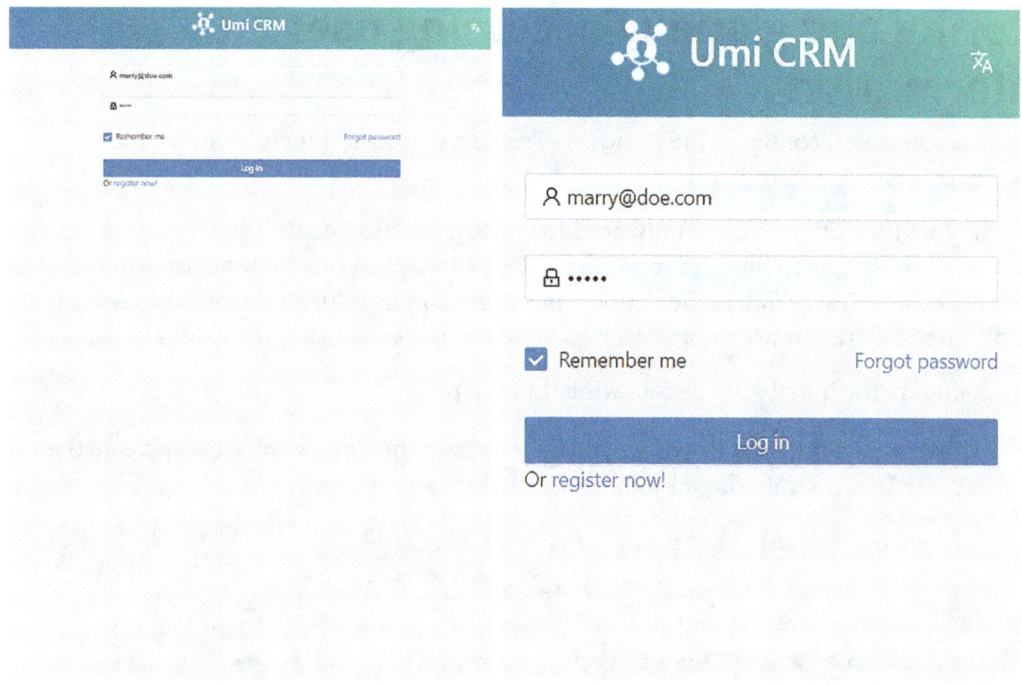

Figure 4.2 – Login page without viewport scale (left side) and with viewport scale (right side)

In this section, we created a Umi mock file and requests to simulate the user authentication. We also modified the login page and defined the viewport scale to correctly display the application's pages on mobile devices by creating the default HTML template for our application.

In the next section, we'll learn how to store and globally access user information after the users log in.

Storing and globally accessing user information

In this section, we'll configure the plugin-initial-state plugin to store and globally access user information.

To configure the initial state, we only need to create a function named getInitialState in the app.tsx file. The getInitialState function will be executed before React renders the entire application, and its return value will be used as the global state. We can use the @@initialState model to access the values.

Let's configure the initial state by following these steps:

1. Create a new file called globalState.d.ts in the types folder, and create the GlobalState interface as follows:

    ```
    import { User } from '@/types/user.d';


    export interface GlobalState {
        login?: (email: string, password: string) =>
          Promise<User>;
        logout?: () => Promise<void>;
        fetchUser?: () => Promise<User>;
        currentUser?: User;
    }
    ```

2. Create the getInitialState function in the app.tsx file located in the src folder as follows:

    ```
    import routes from '../config/routes';
    import { RunTimeLayoutConfig, history } from 'umi';
    import HeaderOptions from './components/HeaderOptions';
    import { getCurrentUser, userLogin, userLogout } from './
    services/user';
    import { GlobalState } from './types/globalState';


    export async function getInitialState():
      Promise<GlobalState> {
      const fetchUser = async () =>
        await getCurrentUser();
    ```

```
const logout = async () => {
  await userLogout(), history.push('/login');
};

const login =
  async (email: string, password: string) => {
  return await userLogin(email, password);
};

const currentUser = await fetchUser();

return {
  login,
  logout,
  fetchUser,
  currentUser,
};
}
```

In the preceding code block, we created functions to log in, log out, fetch user data, and return it as the initial state value.

Now, we can access the user information by reading the currentUser property.

Next, let's read the initial state in the layout header by following these steps:

1. In the index.tsx file, under the src/components folder, read the initial state on the HeaderMenu component as follows:

```
export default function HeaderMenu() {
  const { initialState, setInitialState } =
    useModel('@@initialState');

  const userLogout = () => {
    initialState?.logout?.();

    setInitialState((state) => ({
      ...state,
      currentUser: undefined,
```

```
    }));
  };
```

We created the `userLogout` function to log out and set the `currentUser` state to `undefined`.

2. Now, in the `Menu` component, add the `onClick` event to execute the `userLogout` function when users click on the logout menu item as follows:

```
const options = (
    <Menu className=
        {styles.menu} onClick={userLogout}>
        <Menu.Item key="center">
            <LogoutOutlined /> Logout
        </Menu.Item>
    </Menu>
);
```

3. Finally, add the user's name below the `Avatar` component as follows:

```
return (
    <Dropdown className=
        {styles.dropdown} overlay={options}>
        <span>
            <Avatar size="small" className=
                {styles.avatar} icon={<UserOutlined />} />
            <span className={`${styles.name} anticon`}>
                {initialState?.currentUser?.name}
            </span>
        </span>
    </Dropdown>
);
```

Next, let's read the user information on the home page by following these steps:

1. In the `index.tsx` file under the `pages/Home` folder, read the initial state as follows:

```
const { initialState } = useModel('@@initialState');
```

2. Next, add the user's name, role, and company as follows:

```
<div className={styles.content}>
  <div className={styles.contentTitle}>
    <FormattedMessage id="greetings.hello" />
      {initialState?.currentUser?.name},{' '}
    <FormattedMessage id="greetings.welcome" />.
  </div>
  <div>
    {initialState?.currentUser?.role?.title} |{' '}
    {initialState?.currentUser?.company}
  </div>
</div>
```

We also need to execute the login function on the login page. Follow these steps to develop the login flow:

1. Add the following function to the index.tsx file in the pages/Login/
    LoginForm folder:

```
const { initialState, setInitialState } = useModel('@@
initialState');

const onFinish = async (values: any) => {
  const user = await initialState?.login?.(
    values.username, values.password);

  if (user) {
    setInitialState((state) => ({
      ...state,
      currentUser: user,
    }));
  }
};
```

When the user sends the login form, we execute the login function, and if the login is successful, we save the user information on the initial state.

2. Now, add the following React effect to the `index.tsx` file in the `pages/`
    `Login` folder:

```
const { initialState } = useModel('@@initialState');
```

```
useEffect(() => {
    if (initialState?.currentUser?.isLoggedIn)
        history.push('/');
}, [initialState?.currentUser]);
```

Here, we defined that when the `currentUser` state changes, we redirect the user
to the home page if the login succeeds.

When users log in to the application, we redirect them to the home page, but we
need to turn users back to the login page when they log out and no longer have access
to other pages. We can set this behavior by reading the initial state in the layout
runtime configuration.

Add the following lines to the `onPageChange` function in the `layout` configuration in
the `app.tsx` file:

```
export const layout: RunTimeLayoutConfig = ({ initialState })
=> {
  return {
    routes,
    rightContentRender: () => <HeaderOptions />,
    onPageChange: () => {
      const isLoggedIn =
      initialState?.currentUser?.isLoggedIn;
      const location = history.location.pathname;

      if (!isLoggedIn && location != '/login')
        history.push(`/login`);
    },
  };
};
```

Here, we defined redirecting the user to the login page if the user is not logged in and the
current page is not the login page.

In this section, we configured our application's initial state, read the user information on the home page and in the `MenuHeader` component, and set the login flow by adding some lines to the layout configuration and the login page.

In the next section, we'll learn how to use `plugin-access` to block unauthorized access.

Protecting application routes based on user roles

In this section, we'll configure the Umi `plugin-access` plugin to define user permissions and protect routes and features from unauthorized access.

To configure the access plugin, we must create an `access.ts` file in the `src` folder. The `access.ts` file must export a function that returns an object, and each property of that object must be a Boolean value representing permissions. Consider the following example:

```
export default function (initialState: any) {
  const { access } = initialState;

  return {
    readOnly: access == 'basic',
  };
}
```

In this example, we read the `access` property from the initial state and returned the `readOnly: true` permission if `access` is equal to `basic`.

Let's create an `access.ts` file for our application.

Create a new file called `access.ts` in the `src` folder and create the `default` function as follows:

```
import { GlobalState } from './types/globalState';

export default function (initialState: GlobalState) {
  const { currentUser } = initialState;

  return {
    canAdmin: currentUser?.role?.id == 0,
```

```
  };
}
```

In the preceding code block, we defined the users with `role id` equal to 0 (sales manager) as the application administrators.

Now, to demonstrate how to use the `canAdmin` permission, let's create a new page that only administrators can access by following these steps:

1. Create a new page in the `pages` folder by running the following command:

    ```
    yarn umi g page /Workflow/index --typescript --less
    ```

2. In the `index.tsx` file, add the `ProTable` component as follows:

    ```tsx
    import ProTable from '@ant-design/pro-table';
    import { Button } from 'antd';
    import { PageContainer } from '@ant-design/pro-layout';
    import { PlusOutlined } from '@ant-design/icons';
    import { FormattedMessage } from '@/.umi/plugin-locale/
    localeExports';
    import columns from './columns';

    export default function Page() {

      return (
        <PageContainer>
          <ProTable<any>
            columns={columns}
            dataSource={workflow}
            rowKey="id"
            search={false}
            pagination={{ pageSize: 5 }}
            dateFormatter="string"
            toolBarRender={() => [
              <Button key="button" icon={<PlusOutlined />}
                type="primary">
                <FormattedMessage id="table.new" />
              </Button>,
    ```

```
        ]}
      />
    </PageContainer>
  );
}
```

We created a simple `ProTable` component to list workflow configurations.

3. Next, add the data source to fill `ProTable` as follows:

```
const workflow = [
  {
    id: 0,
    name: 'AssignEmail',
    table: 'Opportunity',
    type: 0,
    trigger: 0,
  },
  {
    id: 1,
    name: 'NewOpportunity',
    table: 'Analytics',
    type: 1,
    trigger: 1,
  },
];
```

4. In the pages/Workflow folder, create a new file called columns.tsx and add the column definitions as follows:

```
import { ProColumns } from '@ant-design/pro-table';
import { FormattedMessage } from 'umi';

const columns: ProColumns<any>[] = [
  {
    title: <FormattedMessage id="table.workflow.name"
            />,
    dataIndex: 'name',
  },
```

```
  {
    title: <FormattedMessage id="table.workflow.type"
          />,
    dataIndex: 'type',
  },
  {
    title: <FormattedMessage id="table.workflow.table"
          />,
    dataIndex: 'table',
  },
  {
    title: <FormattedMessage id="table.options" />,
    valueType: 'option',
    hideInSetting: true,
    hideInDescriptions: true,
    render: () => [
      <a>
        <FormattedMessage id="table.edit" />
      </a>,
    ],
  },
];

export default columns;
```

5. Add the following text to the en-US.ts file in the locales folder:

```
'table.workflow.name': 'Name',
'table.workflow.type': 'Type',
'table.workflow.table': 'Table',
```

6. Now, add the route configuration to the workflow page to the `routes.ts` file as follows:

```
{
    path: '/workflow',
    name: 'workflow',
    access: 'canAdmin',
    icon: 'DeploymentUnitOutlined',
    component: '@/pages/Workflow',
},
```

Notice the `access` property in the route configuration. In the `access` property, we can set the permissions defined in the `access.ts` file. Now, only users with the sales manager role can access the workflow page.

7. We can also define in the layout configuration a default page to display when users don't have sufficient permissions to access a page. Add the following definition to the layout configuration in the `app.tsx` file:

```
unAccessible: (
  <Result
    status="403"
    title="403"
    subTitle="Sorry, you are not authorized to access
             this page."
    extra={
        <Button type="primary" onClick={() =>
          history.push('/')}>
          Back to Home
        </Button>
    }
  />
)
```

We added the `Result` component from Ant Design to display the unauthorized error page and a button so users can go back to the home page. Here's how the page will look:

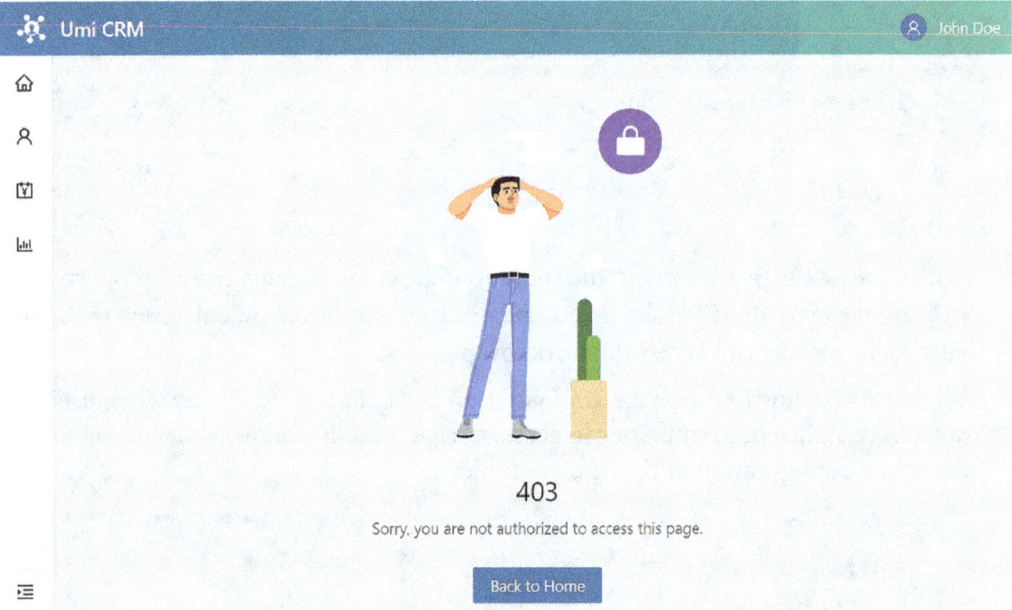

Figure 4.3 – Unauthorized error page

We have now created the `access.ts` file and used the `canAdmin` permission to protect the workflow page. Next, we'll learn how to use permissions to protect other application features.

Using the useAccess hook

We can use the permissions we created in the `access.ts` file to authorize users to execute any actions in our application using the `useAccess` hook and the `Access` component. Consider the following example:

```
import { useAccess } from "umi";


const Page = (props) => {
  const [disabled, setDisabled] = useState<any>();
  const access = useAccess();


  if (access.readOnly) {
```

```
        setDisabled(true);
  }


  return <Button disabled={disabled}> Edit </Button>;
};


export default Page;
```

In this example, we read the `readOnly` permission to define whether the **Edit** button will be disabled.

Now, consider another example using the `Access` component:

```
import { useAccess } from "umi";


const Page = (props) => {
  const access = useAccess();


  return (
    <Access
      accessible={access.readAndWrite}
      fallback={<div>You are not allowed to write
              content.</div>}
    >
      <TextArea></TextArea>
    </Access>
  );
};


export default Page;
```

In this example, we'll render the content in the `fallback` property if the user doesn't have the `readAndWrite` permission instead of rendering the `TextArea` component.

Let's use the `useAccess` hook to allow administrators to assign an opportunity to an inside sales representative by following these steps:

1. Add the following line to the `index.tsx` file in the `pages/Opportunities` folder to read the `canAdmin` permission:

    ```
    const { canAdmin } = useAccess();
    ```

2. Next, add the following properties to the `ProTable` component:

    ```
    rowSelection={canAdmin && { onChange: () => {} }}
    tableAlertOptionRender={() => <a>Assign</a>}
    ```

We defined that only if the user has the `canAdmin` permission, we'll apply the `onChange` event, enabling the `ProTable` row selection.

Now, if the user is an administrator, they can assign an opportunity as shown in the following screenshot:

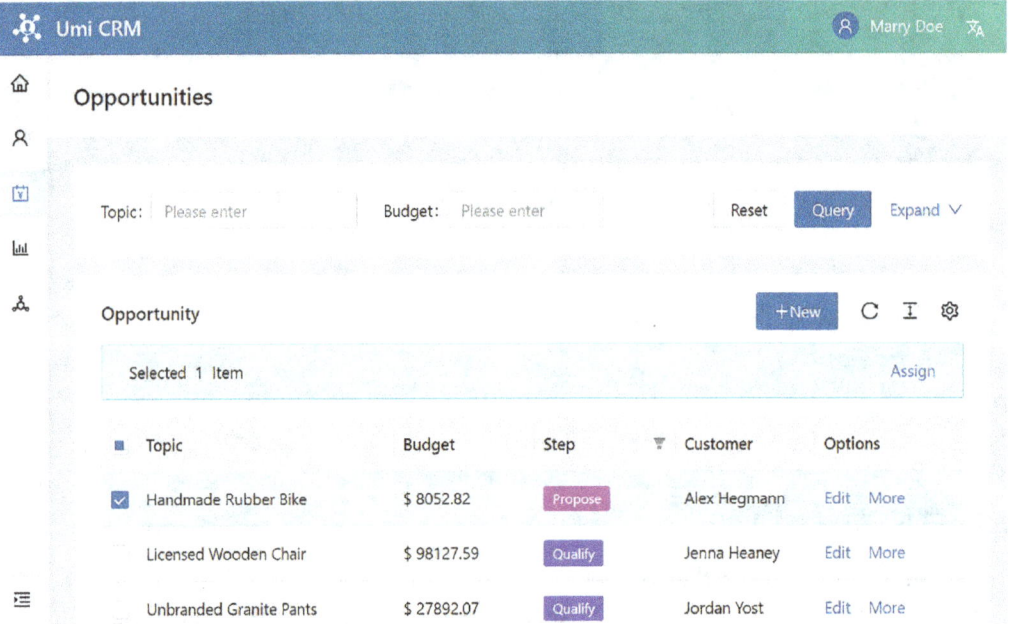

Figure 4.4 – Assign opportunity feature

In this section, we created the `access.ts` file and defined the administrator permissions based on the user role. Then, we used the `canAdmin` permission to block unauthorized access to the workflow page and the row selection feature.

In the next section, you'll learn how to handle HTTP error responses by configuring the umi-request library.

Handling HTTP error responses

In this section, we'll configure the umi-request library to handle error responses and display visual feedback.

We'll use the `errorHandler` function, one of the many umi-request library configurations. I recommend you read the documentation available at `https://github.com/umijs/umi-request` to learn more about other features.

The umi-request library will trigger the `errorHandler` function every time it receives an HTTP error response, and we will read the response status and show a message to inform the user why the action they tried to execute failed.

Follow these steps to configure the umi-request library:

1. In the `app.tsx` file, create a new function and add the `request` configuration as follows:

```tsx
const errorHandler = (error: ResponseError) => {
  const { response } = error;
  let messages = undefined;

  switch (getLocale()) {
    case 'en-US':
      messages = eng;
      break;
    case 'pt-BR':
      messages = port;
      break;
  }

  if (response) {
    message.error(messages[response.status]);
  } else if (!response) {
    message.error(messages['empty']);
  }
}
```

```
      throw error;
   };
```

```
   export const request: RequestConfig = { errorHandler };
```

We used the `getLocale()` function from Umi to define in what language we'll display the messages. Next, we displayed an error message based on the response status or empty response and exported the request configuration with the `errorHandler` function.

2. Next, we need to define the messages. In the `src/locales` folder, under the `en-US` folder, create a new file called `http.ts` and add the following messages:

```
export default {
    400: 'The request failed.',
    401: 'Invalid credentials, you are not
           authenticated.',
    403: 'You cannot perform this operation.',
    404: 'Resource not found.',
    405: 'Operation not allowed.',
    406: 'The operation cannot be completed.',
    410: 'The service is no longer available',
    422: 'Could not process your request.',
    500: 'Internal error, contact administrator.',
    502: 'Internal service communication failed.',
    503: 'Service temporarily unavailable.',
    504: 'The maximum wait time for an answer has
           expired.',
  empty: 'Failed to connect to services',
   };
```

You also need to download the Portuguese version of the `http.ts` file available in the GitHub repository of this book and place it in the `locales/pt-BR` folder.

3. Now, import the `http.ts` file from the `en-US` and `pt-BR` folders in the `app.ts` file as follows:

```
import eng from './locales/en-US/http';
import port from './locales/pt-BR/http';
```

When the Umi request receives an HTTP error response, the user will see a message as shown in the following screenshot:

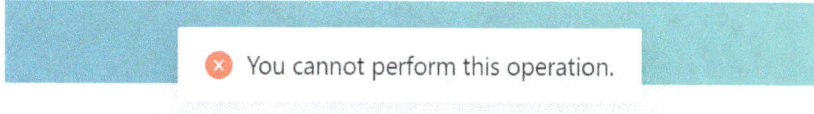

Figure 4.5 – Feedback message on failed request

In this section, we configured the umi-request library to handle HTTP error responses and display a feedback message to inform the user what happened.

Summary

In this chapter, we created the login page and the document.ejs file, and learned how to set the viewport scale to display our pages on mobile devices correctly. You learned how to store and globally access data by configuring the initial state plugin and reading the initial state properties on the login and home page.

We created user permissions by configuring the access plugin and created the workflow page on which we blocked unauthorized access using the access plugin. We enabled the ProTable row selection feature only for authorized users using the access plugin.

Finally, we configured the umi-request library to handle HTTP error responses and display feedback messages to inform users what happened.

In the next chapter, you'll learn about code style, formatting, and how to improve your code using **linters** and formatting tools.

5
Code Style and Formatting Tools

In addition to meeting business requirements, a professional frontend project should feature clean source code that is easy to maintain and extend.

In this chapter, we'll discuss code style and consistency. Next, you'll learn how to use **Prettier** and **EditorConfig** to enforce standard code formatting in teams with multiple members working with various **integrated development environments (IDEs)** and editors. Finally, we'll add **ESLint** to our project and configure it to work with Prettier and improve your code quality.

In this chapter, we'll cover the following main topics:

- Understanding code style and consistency
- Working with EditorConfig and Prettier
- Configuring ESLint and Prettier

By the end of this chapter, you'll have learned how to configure Prettier and EditorConfig, avoiding conflicts and redundancy. You'll also have learned how to configure ESLint to improve the code quality and Prettier to format the code in the same project, avoiding conflicts between these two tools.

Technical requirements

To complete this chapter's exercises, you only need a computer with any OS (I recommend Ubuntu 20.04 or higher) and the software installed in *Chapter 1, Environment Setup and Introduction to UmiJS* (VS Code, Node.js, and Yarn).

You can find the complete project in the `Chapter05` folder in the GitHub repository available at `https://github.com/PacktPublishing/Enterprise-React-Development-with-UmiJs`.

Understanding code style and consistency

In this section, we'll discuss code style with some examples, so you will be able to understand why it's essential to use tools such as **Prettier**, **EditorConfig**, and **ESLint** when working on large enterprise projects.

We will not discuss JavaScript code conventions, but if you want to revise this topic, I recommend you read the *Mozilla Developer Network JavaScript Guidelines* at `https://developer.mozilla.org/en-US/docs/MDN/Guidelines/Code_guidelines/JavaScript`.

Each developer has their preferences when deciding how to format code. Even when following a specific language convention, some decisions about the code formatting can divide developers. Consider the following function invocation example:

```
function execute(param1, param2, param3) {
    return param1 + param2 + param3;
}


execute(arg1, arg2, arg3);
```

Here, we invoke the function by passing the arguments inline. In some cases, when passing more arguments, you may need to break down the function call, and you can do that in different ways. Consider the following example:

```
// Style 1 - Hug paren
execute(
    arg1,
    arg2,
    arg3);

// Style 2 - Align paren
execute(arg1,
    arg2,
    arg3);

// Style 3 - Inner arguments
execute(
    arg1,
    arg2,
    arg3
);
```

Figure 5.1 – Breaking down a function call in three different styles

Here, we broke down the same function call using three distinct styles: hug the last parenthesis, align the parentheses, and align the arguments. Now imagine that the first argument is another function call; the complexity starts to grow. Consider another example:

```
// Style 1 - Break inner function
execute(execute(
    arg1,
    arg2,
    arg3), arg2, arg3);

// Style 2 - Break outer function
execute(
    execute(arg1, arg2, arg3),
    arg2,
    arg3
);

// Style 3 - Break both functions
execute(
    execute(
        arg1,
        arg2,
        arg3
    ),
    arg2,
    arg3
);
```

Figure 5.2 – Breaking down functions and inner functions

Here, we broke down the function and inner function calls using three different code styles. You may have noticed that each approach drastically changes the code style. As more developers work on the code and use different styles, the code base will become unclean, unprofessional, and hard to read.

Some of the style decisions can also make the code harder to understand. Consider the following example:

```
// Style 1 - No parentheses
a && b || c && d ? <div>...</div> : null

// Style 2 - With parentheses
(a && b) || (c && d) ? <div>...</div> : null
```

Figure 5.3 – Conditional ternary operator with and without parentheses

Here, we used the conditional ternary operator with two different styles: without parentheses and enclosing with parentheses. Using parentheses in complex conditions makes the code easier to read and understand.

The professional approach to developing clean and consistent code when working with large projects and multiple team members is to define a standard code style that every developer must follow. The code style should be discussed and documented so that every developer knows how to use it. This approach introduces other challenges, however, as we need to ensure that all developers follow the code style. Probably, you will end up reviewing the code to fix code style issues, which is a waste of time and money as it doesn't deliver value to the customer.

To avoid spending time reviewing code only to fix code style issues, we can use formatting tools that enforce the code style.

You can use numerous tools to enforce code style and consistency in JavaScript projects. In the coming sections, we will focus on three tools that solve the problems mentioned previously. We will look at the following three tools:

- Prettier, a formatting tool that can parse and format JavaScript, LESS style sheets, JSX components, and more

- EditorConfig, a tool for enforcing a default code format that almost any IDE can follow

- ESLint, a tool for formatting and fixing code and finding quality-related issues

In this section, we discussed different code styles by seeing examples and understanding why we need to implement tools and strategies to enforce a consistent code style when working on large projects with multiple team members.

Now, let's take a closer look at Prettier and EditorConfig to see how these two tools can work together to solve the code style problem.

Working with EditorConfig and Prettier

In this section, you'll learn how **Prettier** and **EditorConfig** can work together to enforce the code style across IDEs and developers' code and how to prevent redundancy when configuring these tools.

Let's start by learning how EditorConfig works.

Working with EditorConfig

EditorConfig consists of a format file and a set of plugins that ensure almost any IDE or editor follows the code style you have defined as you type. In some cases, you don't even need to install any extensions as various IDEs and editors come with native support for EditorConfig. You can read more about EditorConfig at `https://editorconfig.org/`.

Let's take the example of the format file that comes with the **umi-app** template, which we used to start our project from scratch:

.editorconfig

```
root = true

[*]
indent_style = space
indent_size = 2
end_of_line = lf
charset = utf-8
trim_trailing_whitespace = true
insert_final_newline = true

[*.md]
trim_trailing_whitespace = false

[Makefile]
indent_style = tab
```

We used the following options in our project:

- `root`: We used this option to tell EditorConfig that we are in the `root` folder, and it doesn't need to search for `.editorconfig` files in any other folders.

- `[*]`: We used this wildcard pattern to apply the following options to every file in the project.

- `indent_style`: We used this option to define indentation using spaces instead of tabs.

- `indent_size`: We used this option to define two spaces for indentation.

- `end_of_line`: This option sets which control character we want to use to mark a line break. We choose the **line feed** (**LF**) character (0x0A).

  The default control character can vary depending on the IDE or editor. Also, IDEs don't render this kind of character, so it's essential to use this option to ensure consistency across IDEs.

- `charset`: We used this option to define the character set as `utf-8`.

- `trim_trailing_whitespace`: We set this option to `true` to remove any whitespace characters before new lines.

- `insert_final_newline`: We used this option to ensure all files end with a new line.

- `[*.md]`: We used this wildcard pattern to apply the following option to the `README.md` file and other documentation defined using markdown.

- `trim_trailing_whitespace`: We set this option to `false` to ensure whitespaces exist before new lines.

- `[Makefile]`: We used this wildcard pattern to apply the following option to any `Makefile` present in the project.

  We usually create commands and logic in `Makefile` and use the **make** utility to build and compile the application.

  You can read more about this tool at: `https://www.gnu.org/software/make/`.

- `indent_style`: Here, we used this option to define the indentation using tabs.

As you may have noticed, we can control every critical aspect of the code style and customize the formatting for each resource type in our project using EditorConfig. All this configuration works across IDEs and editors so that the code style will be consistent no matter what the developers' preferences are.

Next, we'll see Prettier, another tool that works well with EditorConfig, to enforce the code style and consistency.

Working with Prettier

Prettier is a code formatting tool that supports numerous JavaScript frameworks, style sheet extensions, markup languages, and configuration files.

As you know, we have been using Prettier since *Chapter 1, Environment Setup and Introduction to UmiJS*. We configured VS Code to use Prettier to format the code on saving and pasting.

In our project, EditorConfig and Prettier share the responsibility to enforce the code style but with different approaches. While EditorConfig overrides the code style of the IDE or editor and ensures that the code is correctly formatted as you type, Prettier applies a standard code style after the developer types the code, replacing the styles with a standard code style defined by Prettier.

When using Prettier, the developer doesn't need to worry about following a specific code style; they can focus on defining interfaces and developing business rules. Prettier will do the job of formatting the code with a consistent code style, and almost all debates about the team's code style are no longer necessary.

Although Prettier doesn't require a lot of configurations, there are some options we can define in the .prettierrc file. Let's take a closer look at our project's configuration:

.prettierrc

```
{
    "singleQuote": true,
    "trailingComma": "all",
    "printWidth": 80,
    "overrides": [
        {
            "files": ".prettierrc",
            "options": { "parser": "json" }
        }
    ]
}
```

These are the options defined in the `.prettierrc` file:

- `singleQuote`: We used this option to use single quotes instead of double quotes in our code, except when writing in JSX files, which skip this option and use double quotes.

- `trailingComma`: We used this option to print trailing commas wherever possible in our code.

- `printWidth`: We used this option to define the maximum line length before Prettier breaks the line.

- `overrides`: This option is similar to the wildcard pattern from EditorConfig. In this option, we can override the options for specific files. Here, we configured Prettier to use the `JSON parser` specifically for the `.prettierrc` file.

The options you can set in `.prettierrc` are limited because Prettier enforces its standard code style. You can find other options in the Prettier documentation at `https://prettier.io/docs/en/options.html`.

When using Prettier and EditorConfig in the same project, you need to avoid setting redundant options between these two tools. A good approach is to put only relevant options to override IDE and editor code style in the `.editorconfig` file and ensure that you are not repeating these options in the `.prettierrc` file.

You can see that, in our project, all the configurations in EditorConfig are different to the configurations in Prettier.

Prettier will parse the `.editorconfig` file to follow its configuration when formatting the code. As the IDE already formatted the code by following the EditorConfig rules, Prettier can skip those rules and apply its own code style rules.

In this section, we learned how to configure EditorConfig by defining code style rules in the `.editorconfig` file and Prettier by defining rules in the `.prettierrc` file. We also learned how to avoid redundancy when working with these tools together.

Next, we'll add ESLint to the project, an essential tool that complements EditorConfig and Prettier in improving the code quality.

Configuring ESLint and Prettier

In this section, we'll configure **ESLint** and integrate Prettier with ESLint to improve the code quality, and to prevent conflicts between these two tools.

ESLint is a tool for analyzing, fixing, and reporting inconsistencies and issues that can generate bugs in your code. This tool can format and improve the code quality with various plugins that implement the rules that meet your project's needs. You can read more about ESLint at `https://eslint.org/`.

Like Prettier and EditorConfig, ESLint also applies style rules to the code. In our scenario, where we use EditorConfig to override the IDE code style and Prettier to enforce a consistent code style by applying its own rules, we'll use only the code quality rules that ESLint offers. We could use only ESLint for code quality and formatting, but Prettier excels in code formatting and easily integrates with ESLint.

Before getting into the details about integrating Prettier and ESLint, let's install and configure ESLint by following these steps:

1. Install ESLint by running the following command:

    ```
    yarn add eslint -D
    ```

2. Next, run the following command to configure ESLint:

    ```
    yarn create @eslint/config
    ```

3. For the first question, **How would you like to use ESLint?**, select the **To check syntax and find problems** option in the terminal and press *Enter*:

    ```
    ? How would you like to use ESLint? ...
      To check syntax only
    > To check syntax and find problems
      To check syntax, find problems, and enforce code style
    ```

    Figure 5.4 – ESLint configuration – How would you like to use ESLint?

4. For the second question, **What type of modules does your project use?**, select the **JavaScript modules (import/export)** option in the terminal and press *Enter*:

```
√ How would you like to use ESLint? · problems
? What type of modules does your project use? ...
> JavaScript modules (import/export)
  CommonJS (require/exports)
  None of these
```

Figure 5.5 – ESLint configuration – What type of modules does your project use?

5. For the third question, **Which framework does your project use?**, select the **React** option and press *Enter*:

```
√ How would you like to use ESLint? · problems
√ What type of modules does your project use? · esm
? Which framework does your project use? ...
> React
  Vue.js
  None of these
```

Figure 5.6 – ESLint configuration – Which framework does your project use?

6. For the fourth question, **Does your project use TypeScript?**, select the **Yes** option and press *Enter*:

```
√ How would you like to use ESLint? · problems
√ What type of modules does your project use? · esm
√ Which framework does your project use? · react
? Does your project use TypeScript? » No / Yes
```

Figure 5.7 – ESLint configuration – Does your project use TypeScript?

7. For the fifth question, **Where does your code run?**, select **Browser** and press *Enter*:

```
√ How would you like to use ESLint? · problems
√ What type of modules does your project use? · esm
√ Which framework does your project use? · react
√ Does your project use TypeScript? · No / Yes
? Where does your code run? ...   (Press <space> to sel

√ Browser
√ Node
```

Figure 5.8 – ESLint configuration – Where does your code run?

8. For the sixth question, **What format do you want your config file to be in?**, select **JSON** and press *Enter*:

```
√ How would you like to use ESLint? · problems
√ What type of modules does your project use? · esm
√ Which framework does your project use? · react
√ Where does your code run? · browser
? What format do you want your config file to be in? ...
  JavaScript
  YAML
> JSON
```

Figure 5.9 – ESLint configuration – What format do you want your config file to be in?

9. For the seventh question, **Would you like to install them now with npm?**, select **No** and press *Enter* as we'll use Yarn instead of npm:

```
√ How would you like to use ESLint? · problems
√ What type of modules does your project use? · esm
√ Which framework does your project use? · react
√ Where does your code run? · browser
√ What format do you want your config file to be in? · JSON
The config that you've selected requires the following dependencies:

eslint-plugin-react@latest @typescript-eslint/eslint-plugin@latest @ty
? Would you like to install them now with npm? » No / Yes
```

Figure 5.10 – ESLint configuration – Would you like to install them (dependencies) now with npm?

10. Next, we need to install the dependencies required by running the following command:

```
yarn add -D eslint-plugin-react@latest @typescript-
eslint/eslint-plugin@latest @typescript-eslint/parser@
latest
```

11. Finally, let's add the VS Code extension to integrate ESLint. Press *Ctrl + P*, type the following command, and press *Enter*:

```
ext install dbaeumer.vscode-eslint
```

After following the preceding steps, a new file called `.eslintrc.json` should exist in our project with the ESLint configuration. Let's take a closer look at those configurations:

.eslintrc.json

```json
{
    "env": {
        "browser": true,
        "es2021": true
    },
    "extends": [
        "eslint:recommended",
        "plugin:react/recommended",
        "plugin:@typescript-eslint/recommended"
    ],
    "parser": "@typescript-eslint/parser",
    "parserOptions": {
        "ecmaFeatures": {
            "jsx": true
        },
        "ecmaVersion": "latest",
        "sourceType": "module"
    },
    "plugins": [
        "react",
        "@typescript-eslint"
    ],
```

```
    "rules": {}
}
```

These are the options defined in the `.eslintrc.json` file:

- `env`: This option defines the global variable. Here, ESLint declares that we are working in the browser and using ECMAScript 2021.

- `extends`: We can extend other configuration files or plugin configurations with this option. Here, ESLint extends its recommended rules, `react` plugin rules, and `typescript-eslint` plugin rules.

- `parser` and `parserOptions`: With these options, we can define what code parser to use and define the parser options. Here, ESLint sets the parser to TypeScript using the `typescript-eslint` package and enables the JSX option.

- `plugins`: With this option, we can set ESLint plugins. Here, ESLint uses the `react` and `typescript-eslint` plugins.

- `rules`: With this option, we can modify the ESLint rules to meet our project's needs.

We want Prettier and EditorConfig working on the code style and ESLint working on the code quality, so we need to disable the ESLint formatting rules. This approach will also prevent conflicts between Prettier and ESLint. Follow these steps to disable the ESLint formatting rules:

1. Install the configurations to disable the ESLint style rules by running the following command:

```
yarn add -D eslint-config-prettier
```

2. Now, install the Prettier ESLint plugin by running the following command:

```
yarn add -D eslint-plugin-prettier
```

3. Finally, extend the Prettier plugin's recommended configurations as follows:

```
"extends": [
    "eslint:recommended",
    "plugin:react/recommended",
    "plugin:@typescript-eslint/recommended",
    "plugin:prettier/recommended"
],
```

Notice that we extended the Prettier plugin's configuration as the last element in the `extends` array. It's important to follow this order for ESLint to correctly merge the shared configurations.

If you open any page component, you can see ESLint in action. Let's open the home page component located in the `index.tsx` file in the `/src/pages/Home` folder.

```
19    useEffect(() => {
20      if (result?.success) {
21        message.success(formatMessage({ id: 'messages.success.operation'
22        (alias) const PageContainer: React.FC<PageContainerProps>
23        import PageContainer
24
25      },    'React' must be in scope when using JSX eslint(react/react-
26             in-jsx-scope)
27      re  View Problem    Quick Fix... (Ctrl+.)
28    💡  <PageContainer
29          header={{ title: undefined }}
30          style={{ minHeight: '90vh' }}
31          content={{
32            <div className={styles.pageHeaderContent}>
33              <div className={styles.avatar}>
34                <Avatar
```

Figure 5.11 – ESLint react-in-jsx-scope rule

Notice that ESLint found an error based on the **react-in-jsx-scope** rule: **'React' must be in scope when using JSX**. We don't need to import React on each component when working with Umi, so let's disable this rule. Extend the `jsx-runtime` configuration from the `react` plugin in our ESLint configuration as follows:

```
"extends": [
  "eslint:recommended",
  "plugin:react/recommended",
  "plugin:@typescript-eslint/recommended",
  "plugin:react/jsx-runtime",
  "plugin:prettier/recommended"
],
```

In this section, we installed and configured ESLint to ensure code quality. We also learned how to integrate Prettier with ESLint by disabling the ESLint code style rules and preventing conflicts between these two tools.

Summary

In this chapter, we discussed code style and learned that it is essential to ensure a consistent code style when working on professional projects with multiple team members.

We learned how to use EditorConfig to define a consistent code style across IDEs and editors and maintain the same formatting regardless of developers' preferences. Next, we learned how to work with Prettier to enforce the code style and how to avoid redundancy when working with Prettier and EditorConfig in the same project.

We also installed and configured ESLint to improve the code quality by analyzing and reporting code issues in your project. We disabled the ESLint style rules by installing and extending the Prettier plugin configuration in our ESLint configuration file. Finally, we disabled the **react-in-jsx-scope** rule by extending the corresponding configuration from the ESLint React plugin.

In the next chapter, we'll discuss code tests and learn how to write tests using the **Jest** and **Puppeteer** libraries.

6
Testing Front-End Applications

Testing software is an essential part of software development. We can prevent errors and ensure that new features don't introduce bugs by implementing well-designed tests.

In this chapter, you'll understand software testing by learning how to design integration and end-to-end tests and apply them in the development process. After that, you'll learn how to write tests using **Jest**, a JavaScript test framework focused on simplicity that works well with React. You'll also learn how to test interfaces by simulating user actions with **Puppeteer** and **Headless Chrome**.

In this chapter, we'll cover the following main topics:

- Understanding software testing
- Writing tests with Jest
- Testing interfaces with Puppeteer

By the end of this chapter, you'll have learned how to design integration and end-to-end tests and how to apply them to improve software quality. You'll have learned how to write tests using Jest, a tool to write and run tests in JavaScript projects. You'll also know how to test interfaces with Puppeteer and Headless Chrome.

Technical requirements

To complete this chapter's exercises, you just need a computer with any OS (I recommend Ubuntu 20.04 or higher) and the software installed in *Chapter 1, Environment Setup and Introduction to UmiJS* (Visual Studio Code, Node.js, and Yarn).

You can find the complete project in the `Chapter06` folder in the GitHub repository available at the following link: `https://github.com/PacktPublishing/ Enterprise-React-Development-with-UmiJs`

Understanding software testing

In this section, we'll discuss software testing and how to design **integration** and **end-to-end tests** to ensure your application works as expected.

There are numerous types of software testing, which we can divide into two categories: functional tests, which ensure that functional requirements and specifications are satisfied, and non-functional tests, which focus on testing the behavior and performance of the system. We'll talk about two types of functional tests in this section:

- **Integration tests**: We write this type of test to ensure that different software components integrate and work correctly to deliver the specified feature.

- **End-to-end tests**: We write this type of test to cover complete user flows, ensuring that features satisfy user expectations.

It's important to mention that coding the test is only one task of implementing software testing, and it's not worth it if you don't have solid feature specifications and test plans.

Let's start discussing integration tests.

Understanding integration testing

We perform integration tests to ensure that the different modules present in the application work correctly and communicate to deliver the requested feature.

Let's take our CRM application as an example. We implemented a feature to show the application in different languages by configuring the Umi locale plugin. We could execute an integration test to ensure that the `SelectLang` component works correctly with `plugin-locale` to show the application in the language selected. In that case, we would need to follow these steps:

1. Hover over the user's name in the upper-right corner.
2. Select **English** from the drop-down menu.
3. Check whether the page is in English.

We can manually execute the integration test following a test plan depending on the test strategy. Still, a better option is to write our tests using automated testing tools for repeating the tests, as necessary, with more agility.

We'll learn how to use automated test tools to develop integration and end-to-end tests in the upcoming sections. Next, let's learn more about end-to-end tests.

Understanding end-to-end testing

As the name suggests, an end-to-end test covers the user journey to execute a task from beginning to end. We need to perform the same actions an actual user must perform, validating the system integrity and alignment with requirements.

For example, imagine that our CRM application has a feature to print the report on the reposts page. An end-to-end test to validate this scenario should cover the following steps:

1. Log into the application.
2. Click on the reports menu.
3. Wait for the charts to load and validate whether they were correctly rendered.
4. Click on the print button.
5. Open the generated PDF and validate the report.

As you can see, this type of test involves several steps depending on the complexity of the system and the task. We can perform end-to-end tests manually following a test plan or automate this process using automated testing tools.

End-to-end tests usually require robust testing tools and are written by **quality assurance (QA)** professionals. Still, we can write end-to-end tests during the development phase. This approach will reduce the issues during the QA phase and accelerate the fixing of issues.

We'll learn how to use Puppeteer to write and automate end-to-end tests in the upcoming sections.

Implementing software testing is an extensive subject. If you want to learn more about this topic, I recommend the article at `https://www.ibm.com/topics/software-testing`.

In this section, we discussed software testing by learning how to design integration and end-to-end tests. Next, you'll learn how to write tests in JavaScript projects using Jest.

Writing tests with Jest

In this section, you'll learn how to write tests using the **Jest framework** in JavaScript projects.

Jest is a fast and reliable test framework for JavaScript projects focusing on simplicity. It works with Babel, TypeScript, Node, React, Angular, Vue, and other tools.

After installing it, we can start using Jest without any extra configuration. In our case, we can write a test and run the `test` command configured in our project without even installing Jest, as Umi already provides Jest with the `umi-test` package.

Consider this end-to-end test written with Jest to test the login flow:

```javascript
it('[END_TO_END] Should sucessfully login', async () => {
    const page = await context.newPage();

    await page.goto('http://localhost:8000');
    await page.waitForNavigation();

    await page.type('#username', 'john@doe.com');
    await page.type('#password', 'user');
    await page.click('#loginbtn');

    const loggedUser = await page.waitForSelector('#loggeduser');
    expect(loggedUser).toBeTruthy();
});
```

In this test, all instructions are written inside the `it` method. You can also use the `test` method instead if you want. The difference between these two methods is just semantics.

Here, the `it` method receives two arguments: the first argument is the test name and the second is an async function that executes the test instructions.

Notice the `expect` method combined with the `toBeTruthy` **matcher** that we used to validate that the element with the `loggeduser` ID exists on the page.

We use matchers to test values against different conditions. You can find a complete list of available Jest matchers at `https://jestjs.io/docs/expect`.

Next, you'll see how to organize related tests by creating a test suite.

Understanding the describe method

When writing multiple related tests, you should organize them within a test suite using the `describe` method, as in the following example:

```
describe('Math test suite', () => {
  it('should return 2', () => {
    const value = 1 + 1;

    expect(value).toBe(2);
  });

  it('should return 25', () => {
    const value = 5 * 5;

    expect(value).toBe(25);
  });
});
```

In this example, we used the `describe` method to create a group for two tests related to math problems.

Let's see how we can execute some setup work before and after the entire test suite or each test run.

Executing instructions before and after tests

Sometimes, you'll have some setup to do before running tests, such as initializing a database connection or generating mock data. You can do that by defining the instructions in the `beforeAll` method to execute before all the tests run or the `beforeEach` method to execute instructions before each test run. Consider the following example:

```
describe('Product test suite', () => {
  let connection: DBConnection;
  let product: Product;

  beforeAll(async () => {
    connection = await database.connect();
  });

  beforeEach(async () => {
    product = connection.query(query);
  });

  it('should be greater than 200', async () => {
    expect(product.units).toBeGreaterThan(200);
  });

  it('should be true', async () => {
    expect(product.active).toBeTruthy();
  });
});
```

In this example, before all the tests ran, we opened the database connection, and before each test run, we used the connection to query the product in the database.

Also, in this example, we need to close the database connection after running the test suite. We can do that by adding the `afterAll` method, as shown in the next example:

```
afterAll(() => connection.close());
```

Like the `afterAll` method, you can use the `afterEach` method to execute instructions after each test run.

In this section, you learned how to write tests using the Jest framework. You learned how to create test suites and execute instructions before and after the tests run.

Next, let's learn about Puppeteer and write integration and end-to-end tests for our application.

Testing interfaces with Puppeteer

In this section, you'll learn how to write integration and end-to-end tests using **Puppeteer** and the **Headless Chrome browser**.

Puppeteer is a Node library to control the Chrome, Chromium, or Firefox browser over the DevTools protocol (or remote protocol for Firefox), which makes it an excellent tool for simulating real scenarios during tests.

When we launch a new browser instance, Puppeteer will default to using **Chrome's headless mode**. Chrome's headless mode only includes the browser engine, with no user interface. Puppeteer uses the Chrome DevTools protocol to control the browser.

With Puppeteer, we can take screenshots of the page, test responsiveness by simulating numerous mobile devices, such as tablets and smartphones, and more.

You can learn more about Puppeteer on the document page available at `https://developers.google.com/web/tools/puppeteer`.

We'll write an integration test and an end-to-end test to demonstrate the use of Puppeteer and Jest.

Testing the access and layout plugins

Let's start by installing Puppeteer by running the following command:

```
yarn add -D puppeteer
```

Puppeteer's configuration is as simple as Jest's. By running this command, Puppeteer will install the latest version of the Chromium browser, and we can start using it.

Now, follow these steps to create the integration test:

1. Create a new folder named `tests` in the project's root folder.
2. In the `tests` folder, create a new file named `integration.test.ts`. Jest will execute all files with a name that includes `.test.ts`.

3. In the `integration.test.ts` file, create a test suite, as follows:

```
import puppeteer, { Browser, BrowserContext, Page } from
'puppeteer';

describe('[SUITE] Integration testing', () => {
  let context: BrowserContext;
  let browser: Browser;

  beforeAll(async () => {
    browser = await puppeteer.launch();
  });

  beforeEach(async () => {
    context =
      await browser.createIncognitoBrowserContext();
  });

  afterEach(() => context.close());

  afterAll(() => browser.close());
});
```

Here, before all tests run, we launch Puppeteer and store the instance in the `browser` variable. By default, Puppeteer will launch Chromium in headless mode. Still, you can launch the full browser version by setting the `headless` option, as follows:

```
browser = await puppeteer.launch({ headless: false });
```

By setting the `headless` option to `false`, you can see Puppeteer opening windows and executing the tests.

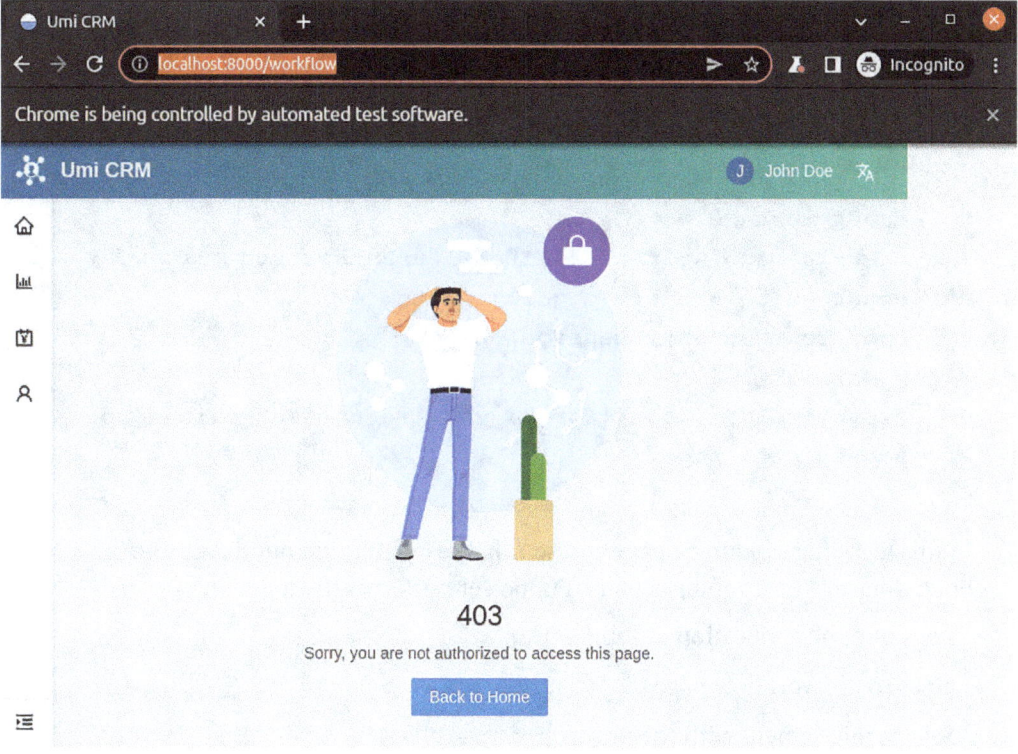

Figure 6.1 – Running an integration test in the full browser version

We create an anonymous browser context by opening an incognito window before each test run to execute them in an isolated environment and store the incognito window in the `context` variable. After each test run, we close the incognito window, and after the entire suite run, we close the browser.

4. You'll notice that TypeScript can't find Jest types. We must install the declaration file by running the following command:

```
yarn add -D @types/jest
```

Now, let's create an integration test to ensure that the Umi access plugin correctly works with the layout plugin to show the 403 error page when unauthorized users try to access a restricted page.

5. Add the following test to the test suite in the `integration.test.ts` file under the `tests` folder:

```
it('[INTEGRATION] Should successfully block unauthorized
access (plugin-access)', async () => {
  const page = await context.newPage();
```

```
page.setDefaultTimeout(10000);

await login(page);
await page.goto('http://localhost:8000/workflow');

const message =
  await page.waitForSelector('#unauthorized');
const value = await page.evaluate((el) =>
  el.textContent, message);

expect(value).toBe('Sorry, you are not authorized to
access this page.');
});
```

In this test, after opening a page and setting the default timeout for `async` operations to `10000` milliseconds, Puppeteer performs the following steps:

- Logs into the application as John Doe
- Goes to the workflow page
- Selects the element with the `unauthorized` ID
- Evaluates the text message inside the element and tests whether the message is correct

Notice that we used the `waitForSelector` method to ensure that the element is already rendered when selecting it.

6. Next, we need to create the `login` function. Add the `login` function before the `describe` method, as follows:

```
async function login(page: Page) {
  await page.goto('http://localhost:8000');
  await page.waitForNavigation();
  await page.type('#username', 'john@doe.com');
  await page.type('#password', 'user');
  await page.click('#loginbtn');
}
```

This function will perform the steps to log in to the application as John Doe. We can reuse the `login` function in other tests within the test suite. Notice we used the `waitForNavigation` method to ensure that the components are rendered before performing the steps.

Now, we need to add the `unauthorized` ID to the element containing the text that we'll validate when running the test.

7. Open the `app.tsx` file located in the `src` folder and modify the layout `unAccessible` configuration option, as follows:

```
unAccessible: (
  <Result
    status="403"
    title="403"
    subTitle={
      <span id="unauthorized">
        Sorry, you are not authorized to access this
        page.
      </span>
    }
    extra={
      <Button type="primary" onClick={() =>
        history.push('/')}>
        Back to Home
      </Button>
    }
  />
),
```

We enclosed the text with a `span` tag containing the `id` property we need.

We also need to add the `id` properties to the login form inputs.

8. Open the `index.tsx` file located under `src/pages/Login/LoginForm` and modify the username input by adding the `username` ID, as follows:

```
<Form.Item
  name="username"
  rules={[
    {
```

```
        required: true,
        message: formatMessage({ id: 'login.alert.username'
}),
      },
  ]}
>
    <Input
      id="username"
      prefix={<UserOutlined className="site-form-item-icon"
        />}
      placeholder={formatMessage({ id: 'login.placeholder.
        username' })}
    />
</Form.Item>
```

9. Next, modify the password input by adding the `password` ID, as follows:

```
<Form.Item
  name="password"
  rules={[
    {
        required: true,
        message: formatMessage({ id: 'login.alert.password'
          }),
      },
  ]}
>
    <Input
      id="password"
      prefix={<LockOutlined className="site-form-item-icon"
        />}
      type="password"
      placeholder={formatMessage({
        id: 'login.placeholder.password' })}
    />
</Form.Item>
```

10. Finally, add the `loginbtn` ID to the login button, as follows:

```
<Form.Item>
  <Button
    id="loginbtn"
    type="primary"
    htmlType="submit"
    className="login-form-button"
  >
    <FormattedMessage id="login.form.login" />
  </Button>
  <FormattedMessage id="login.form.or" />{' '}
  <a href="">
    <FormattedMessage id="login.form.register" />!
  </a>
</Form.Item>
```

You can execute the test by running the `yarn test` command. The result should look as in the following screenshot:

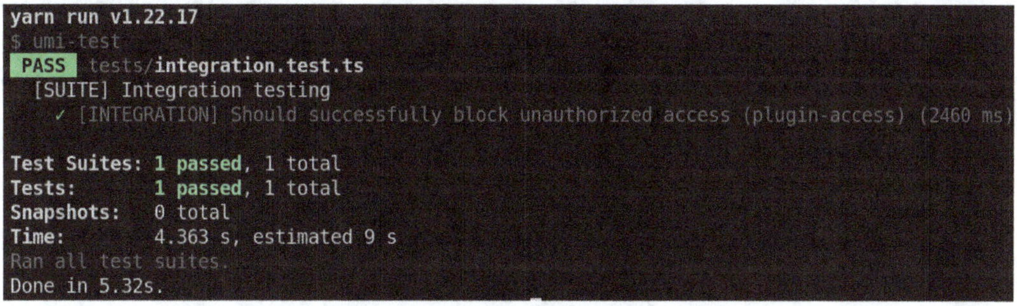

```
yarn run v1.22.17
$ umi-test
 PASS  tests/integration.test.ts
  [SUITE] Integration testing
    ✓ [INTEGRATION] Should successfully block unauthorized access (plugin-access) (2460 ms)

Test Suites: 1 passed, 1 total
Tests:       1 passed, 1 total
Snapshots:   0 total
Time:        4.363 s, estimated 9 s
Ran all test suites.
Done in 5.32s.
```

Figure 6.2 – Integration test result

Now, let's create an end-to-end test to ensure that the feature for editing an opportunity works as expected.

Testing the opportunity editing feature

Follow these steps to create the end-to-end test to ensure the editing feature works as expected on the opportunities page:

1. We'll create a separate file for end-to-end tests. In the `tests` folder, create a file named `end2end.test.ts`, and create the `describe` method, as follows:

    ```
    import puppeteer, { Browser, BrowserContext, Page } from
    'puppeteer';

    describe('[SUITE] End-to-end testing', () => {
      let context: BrowserContext;
      let browser: Browser;

      beforeAll(async () => {
        browser = await puppeteer.launch();
      });

      beforeEach(async () => {
        context =
          await browser.createIncognitoBrowserContext();
      });

      afterEach(() => context.close());

      afterAll(() => browser.close());
    });
    ```

2. Next, add the end-to-end test to the `describe` method, as follows:

    ```
    it('[END_TO_END] Should sucessfully edit opportunity',
    async () => {
      const page = await context.newPage();
      page.setDefaultTimeout(10000);

      await page.goto('http://localhost:8000');
      await page.waitForNavigation();
    });
    ```

We have written the instructions for Puppeteer to open a new page and set the default timeout to 1000, go to the login page, and wait for the page to load.

3. Add the instructions to log into the application, as follows:

```
await page.type('#username', 'john@doe.com');
await page.type('#password', 'user');
await page.click('#loginbtn');

await page.goto('http://localhost:8000/opportunities');
```

Puppeteer will type the user's email address in the input with the username ID and the password in the input with the password ID, then click on the button with the loginbtn ID. Finally, Puppeteer will navigate to the opportunities page.

4. Add the steps to edit the opportunity topic, as follows:

```
await (await page.waitForSelector('#editopportunity')).
click();

const topicInput = await page.$(
  'table > tbody > tr > td > div > div > div > div > span
  > input',
);

await topicInput.click({ clickCount: 3 });
await topicInput.type('Opportunity topic');

await (await page.waitForSelector('#save')).click();
```

Puppeteer will wait for the element with the id equal to editopportunity to be rendered before clicking on it and selecting the text by triple-clicking the input element. Next, Puppeteer will type new text in the topic input and save the opportunity.

5. Now, let's add the steps to evaluate the result, as follows:

```
const topicCell = await page.waitForSelector(
  'tr[data-row-key="0"] > .ant-table-cell',
);

const value = await page.evaluate((el) => el.textContent,
```

```
    topicCell);
```

```
    expect(value).toBe('Opportunity topic');
```

Puppeteer will select the topic cell in the first row of the opportunities table and evaluate its text content. Next, Jest will test the value to ensure it's correct.

6. Finally, let's add the `id` property to the elements we need to find during the test. In the `columns.tsx` file, under the `pages/Opportunities` folder, add the `id` property to the edit option anchor, as follows:

```
{
    title: <FormattedMessage id="table.options" />,
    valueType: 'option',
    hideInSetting: true,
    hideInDescriptions: true,
    render: (_, record, __, action) => [
      <a
        key="editable"
        id="editopportunity"
        onClick={() => {
        action?.startEditable(record.id as number);
      }}
      >
        <FormattedMessage id="table.edit" />
      </a>,
      <a key="more" onClick={() => history.push(`/
      opportunity/${record.id}`)}>
        <FormattedMessage id="table.more" />
      </a>,
    ],
},
```

7. In the `index.ts` file, in the same folder, add the `saveText` property to the editable attribute of the `ProTable` component, as follows:

```
editable={{
    type: 'multiple',
    deletePopconfirmMessage: <FormattedMessage
```

```
        id="table.confirm" />,
      saveText: <span id="save">save</span>,
      deleteText: <FormattedMessage id="table.disable" />,
      onDelete: async (key) => disable(key as string),
      onSave: async (_, record) => update(record),
    }}
```

Before executing the test, let's add the --runInBand flag to the umi-test command in the package.json file, as follows:

```
"test": "umi-test --runInBand",
```

This flag will prevent a race condition between these two tests as we are using the mock API to simulate the backend.

Now, you can execute the test by running the yarn test command. The result should look like the following:

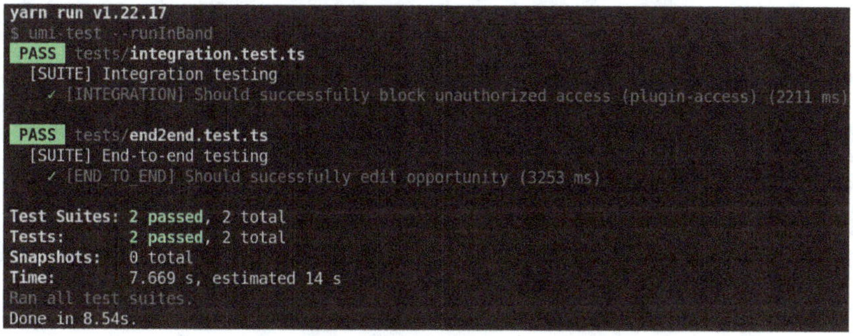

Figure 6.3 – End-to-end test result

In this section, you learned how to write integration tests and end-to-end tests using Puppeteer. To demonstrate the use of Puppeteer with Jest, we created an integration test to ensure the Umi locale plugin works correctly with the layout plugin to render the 403 error page. We also created an end-to-end test to ensure the feature to edit an opportunity works as expected.

Summary

In this chapter, we discussed software testing by learning how to design integration and end-to-end tests. You learned how to use the Jest framework to write tests in React projects. You saw how to use the describe and test (or it) methods to write and organize related tests. You also learned how to execute instructions before and after tests run using the beforeAll, beforeEach, afterAll, and afterEach methods.

You then learned how to write tests using Puppeteer and Headless Chrome by simulating user interaction on your interface. To demonstrate the use of Puppeteer with Jest, we created an integration test to ensure the Umi locale plugin works correctly with the layout plugin and also created an end-to-end test to ensure the feature to edit an opportunity works as expected.

In the next chapter, we will learn how to compile and deploy our applications to online services.

7
Single-Page Application Deployment

In the previous chapter, we discussed software testing and how to write a test and apply it during the development process to prevent errors and improve the software quality.

The last step in the software development life cycle is deploying the application to online services. In this chapter, we'll create a simple mock server as your application's backend using the open source **Mockachino** service. You will learn how to build the application and the compiled source code files generated by Umi. You'll also learn how to deploy and configure your application on **AWS Amplify**.

In this chapter, we'll cover the following main topics:

- Creating a mock server with Mockachino
- Compiling the application and setting environment variables
- Hosting the application on AWS Amplify

By the end of this chapter, you'll have learned how to build the application and the compiled source code files generated by Umi. You'll also know how to use the Mockachino service to create a mock server quickly. You'll also have learned how to deploy and configure single-page applications on AWS Amplify.

Technical requirements

To complete this chapter's exercises, you only need a computer with any OS (I recommend Ubuntu 20.04 or higher) and the software installed in *Chapter 1, Environment Setup and Introduction to UmiJS* (VS Code, Node.js, and Yarn).

You can find the complete project in the Chapter07 folder in the GitHub repository available at https://github.com/PacktPublishing/Enterprise-React-Development-with-UmiJs.

Creating a mock server with Mockachino

In this section, we'll create a mock server using Mockachino to simulate the application's backend services.

Our application is only the presentation layer of the CRM system, where users can visualize and input data. Before deploying it, we need online backend services our application can connect with for processing, storing, and receiving data.

The backend services are APIs and microservices implemented by backend developers to securely and efficiently apply business logic and store information such as opportunities, activities, customers, and user information.

As the objective of this book is to teach React development with UmiJS, we won't build backend services. We'll use **Mockachino** to simulate the backend.

Mockachino is a straightforward service for creating a mock server. We only need to define an endpoint, and Mockachino will provide a space and a secret link to access the space whenever necessary.

Let's start by creating the route to retrieve user information. Navigate to https://www.mockachino.com/ and follow these steps:

1. In the **HTTP Path** field, type api/currentUser.

2. Next, in the **HTTP Response Body** field, type the following JSON response:

```
{
    "company": "Umi Group",
```

```
  "name": "Marry Doe",
  "role": {
    "id": 0,
    "title": "Administrator"
  },
  "isLoggedIn": "true",
  "id": "1"
}
```

3. Click on **Create**, and Mockachino will provide a secret link, as shown in the following screenshot:

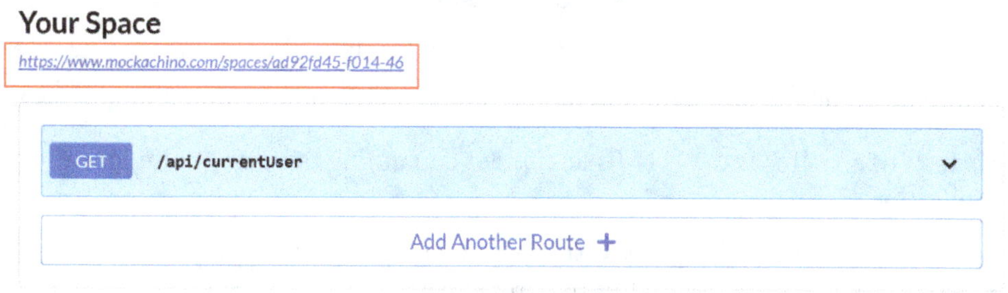

Your Space

https://www.mockachino.com/spaces/ad92fd45-f014-46

| GET | /api/currentUser | ⌄ |

Add Another Route ✛

Figure 7.1 – Mockachino space secret link

By clicking on the endpoint route (**GET /api/currentUser**), you can edit endpoint attributes such as the path, HTTP response headers, and response body.

To create a new route, click on **Add Another Route** and fill the fields with the content available in the mockachino.md file.

For your convenience, I've created a markdown file named mockachino.md in the Chapter07 folder in this book's GitHub repository. In this file, you will find all the routes and the responses you must create in Mockachino before going through the upcoming sections.

In this section, we created a mock server using Mockachino to simulate the backend services. Next, let's learn how to bundle the application and set environment variables.

Compiling the application and setting environment variables

In this section, you'll learn what files Umi will generate and how to compile the application. We'll also set an environment variable to configure the URL for sending HTTP requests.

We need to transform and compile our components and dependencies into a format that web browsers can interpret and render before deploying the application.

Run the `yarn build` command configured in our package scripts. This command will compile the application and place the compiled source code files in the `dist` folder.

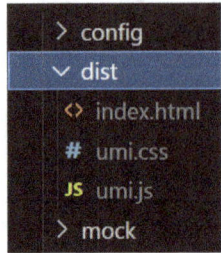

Figure 7.2 – Compiled source code files

You will find three files in the `dist` folder:

- `index.html`: This is the HTML document containing the entry point for our application.
- `umi.css`: This is the compressed style sheet containing all the application styles generated by LESS files present in the project.
- `umi.js`: This is the compressed file containing all the JavaScript code required to execute our application.

Now, we need to host these files on a static server on the internet. When users navigate to the server's public address, the browser will request and receive the `index.html` document, the entry point for our application. We'll host our application on Amplify in the next section.

Now, let's adjust your application to send requests to Mockachino.

Configuring the API URL environment variable

As mentioned earlier, we don't have a mock server running alongside our application in production. We'll send HTTP requests to Mockachino, so we need to change the URL argument in all functions in the `services` folder. We'll do that by configuring an environment variable.

Umi can read environment variables during the build process and use their values in our application; we only need to set the Umi `define` configuration option.

Let's create an environment variable to set the API URL by following these steps:

1. Create a new file named .env in the project's root folder and create a variable called API_URL as follows:

    ```
    API_URL=https://www.mockachino.com/secret
    ```

    Replace the value with the URL provided by Mockachino.

2. Add the define option to the configuration in the config.ts file as follows:

    ```
    define: {
        API_URL: process.env.API_HOST,
    },
    ```

    This configuration defines the API_URL variable in the project.

3. Now, let's create a file to export the variable and prevent TypeScript warnings. Create a new file called env.ts in the config folder and export the variable as follows:

    ```
    // @ts-nocheck
    export default {
        API_URL: API_URL,
    };
    ```

4. In the user.ts file in the src/services folder, import the env.ts file as follows:

    ```
    import env from '../../config/env';
    ```

5. Next, add API_URL to the first argument of the request function as follows:

    ```
    return request<User>(`${env.API_URL}/api/currentUser`, {
        method: 'GET',
        headers: { 'Content-Type': 'application/json' },
        params: { context: contextId },
    });
    ```

Follow the last two steps to change all the request functions in all files in the services folder.

In this section, you learned how to compile our application's source code files and what files Umi generates during the build process. We also created an environment variable and changed the requests to use Mockachino as the backend.

Now, we'll host our application on AWS using the Amplify Console services.

Hosting the application on AWS Amplify

In this section, you'll learn how to deploy and configure single-page applications on **Amazon Web Services (AWS)** by hosting our application using Amplify Console.

AWS Amplify is a flexible set of tools for web and mobile frontend developers to create and deploy applications on AWS using various services. With Amplify, you can quickly build and deploy a full stack application without having to research and learn individual AWS services.

We'll use Amplify only to host our application, but you can create backend services and add authentication, artificial intelligence, machine learning, and more using the Amplify framework and Amplify Studio. If you want to know more, visit the framework's documentation page at `https://docs.amplify.aws/`.

Before proceeding to the following steps, you need to push the project to a new repository in your personal GitHub account.

Also, you need to create a free AWS account. Visit `https://aws.amazon.com/free`, click on **Create a Free Account**, and fill in the form with the required information to create your account.

Now, after pushing the code to a new repository and creating your AWS account, follow these steps to host our application on Amplify:

1. Navigate to `http://console.aws.amazon.com/amplify/home` and sign in to your AWS account.

2. Click on the menu highlighted in the following screenshot and, after that, click on **All apps**:

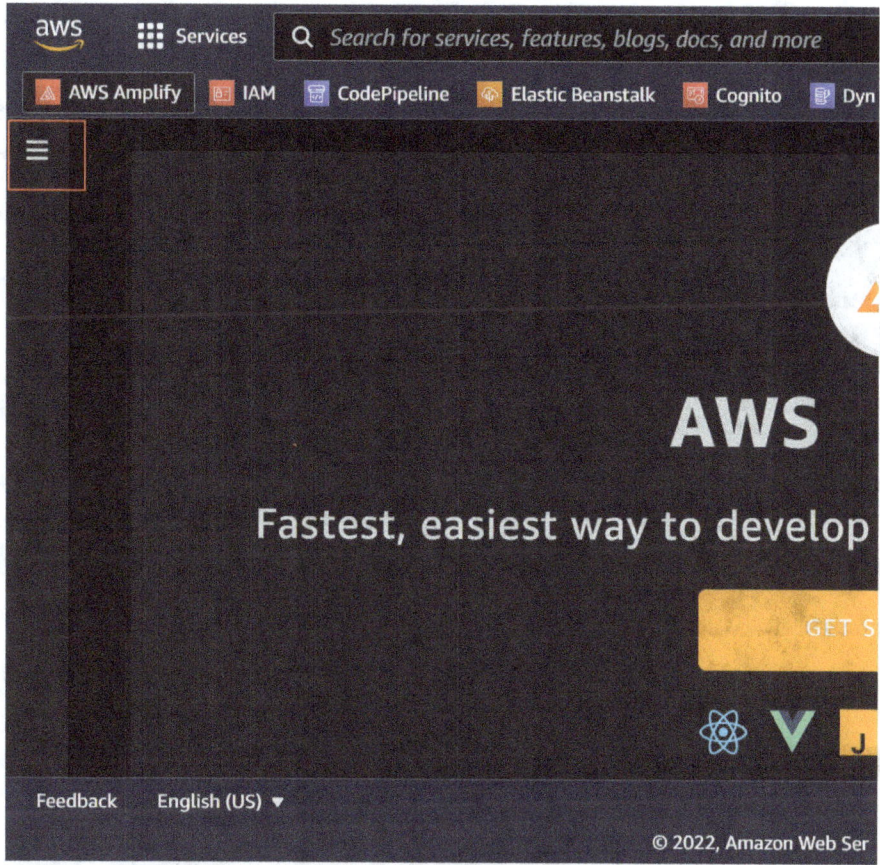

Figure 7.3 – Left-side menu

3. At the top right of the page, click on the **New app** dropdown and select **Host web app**:

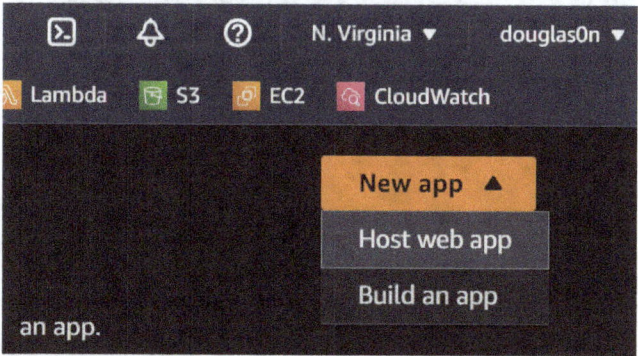

Figure 7.4 – Host web app option

4. Now, select **GitHub** in the **From your existing code** section, click on **Continue**, and sign in to your GitHub account:

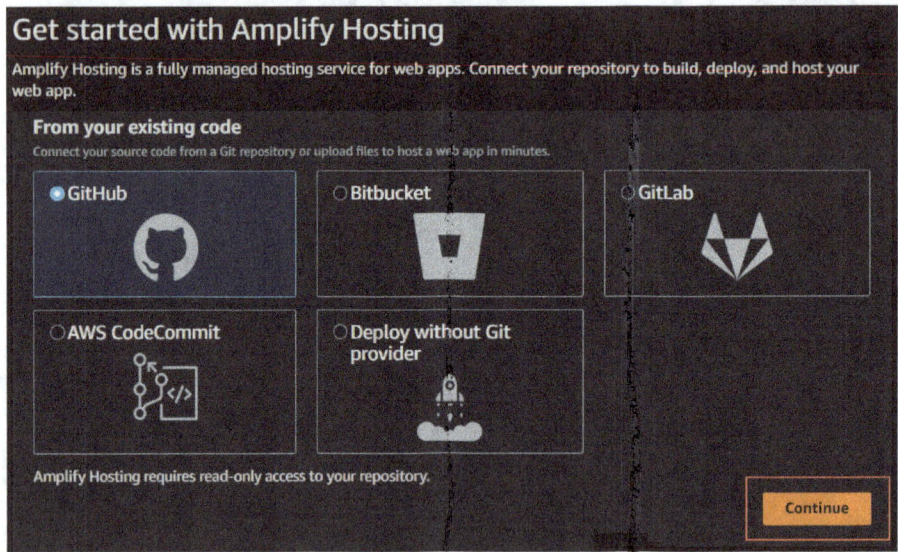

Figure 7.5 – Selecting a source Git provider

5. Next, select the repository you created for our project and click on **Next**:

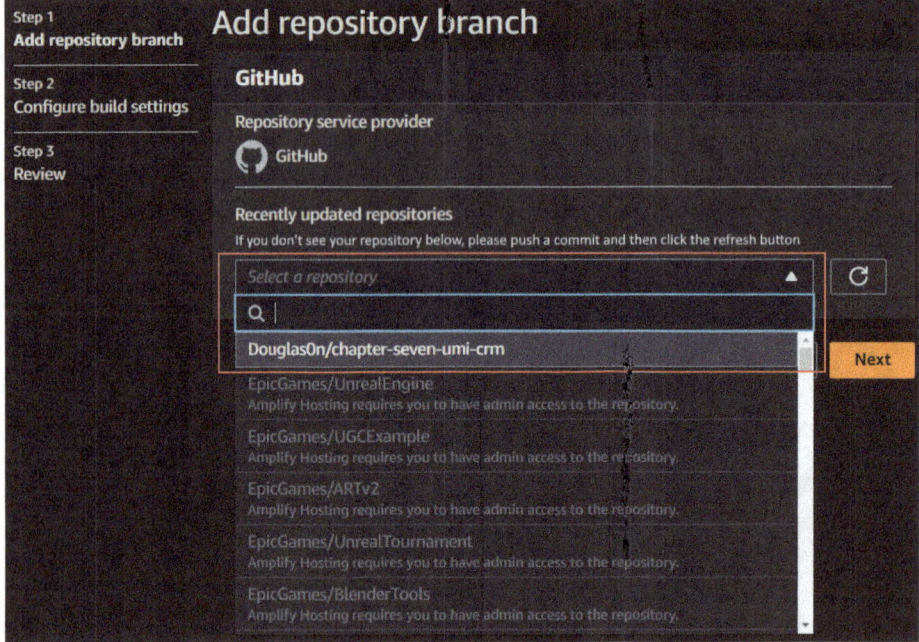

Figure 7.6 – Selecting a GitHub repository

6. In **Step 2 Configure build settings**, in the **Build and test settings** section, click on **Edit**, modify line 12 as follows, and click on **Save**:

```
baseDirectory: /dist
```

This configuration will set where Amplify looks for source code when running the automated pipeline.

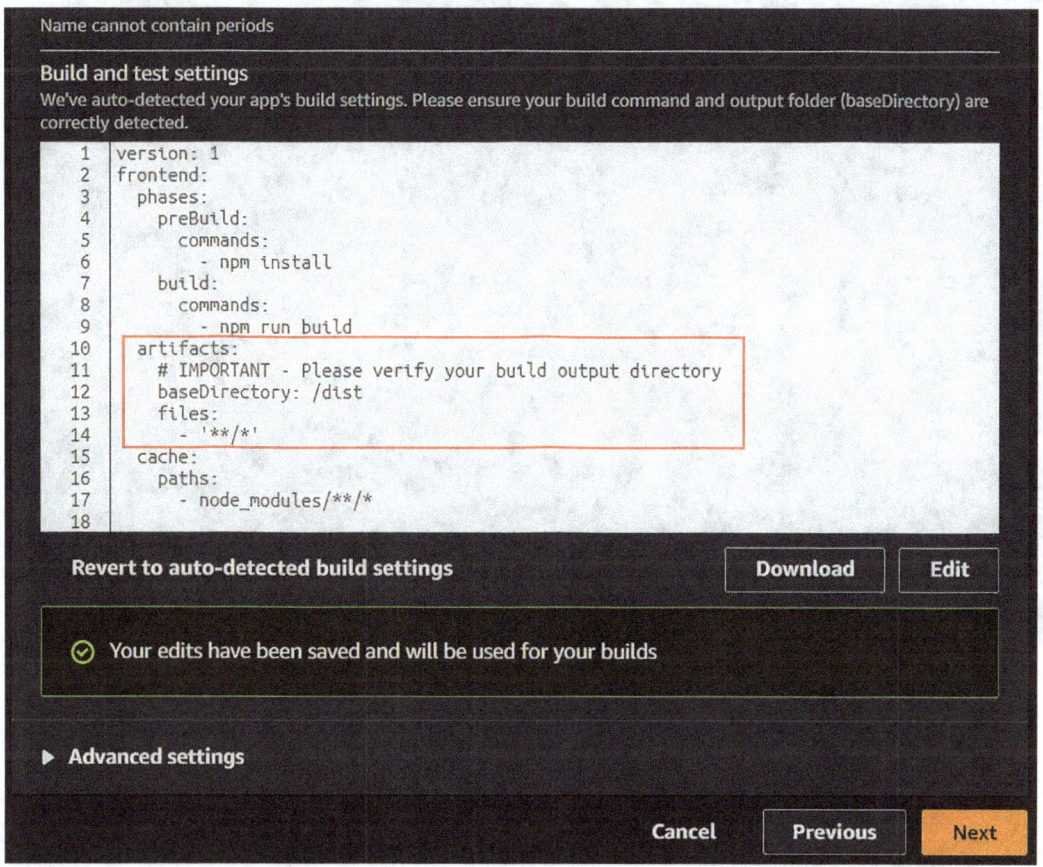

Figure 7.7 – Configuring the source code base directory

7. Click on **Advanced settings** and, in the **Environment variables** section, create a new variable. In the **Key** field, type API_URL, and then paste the Mockachino secret link in the **Value** field:

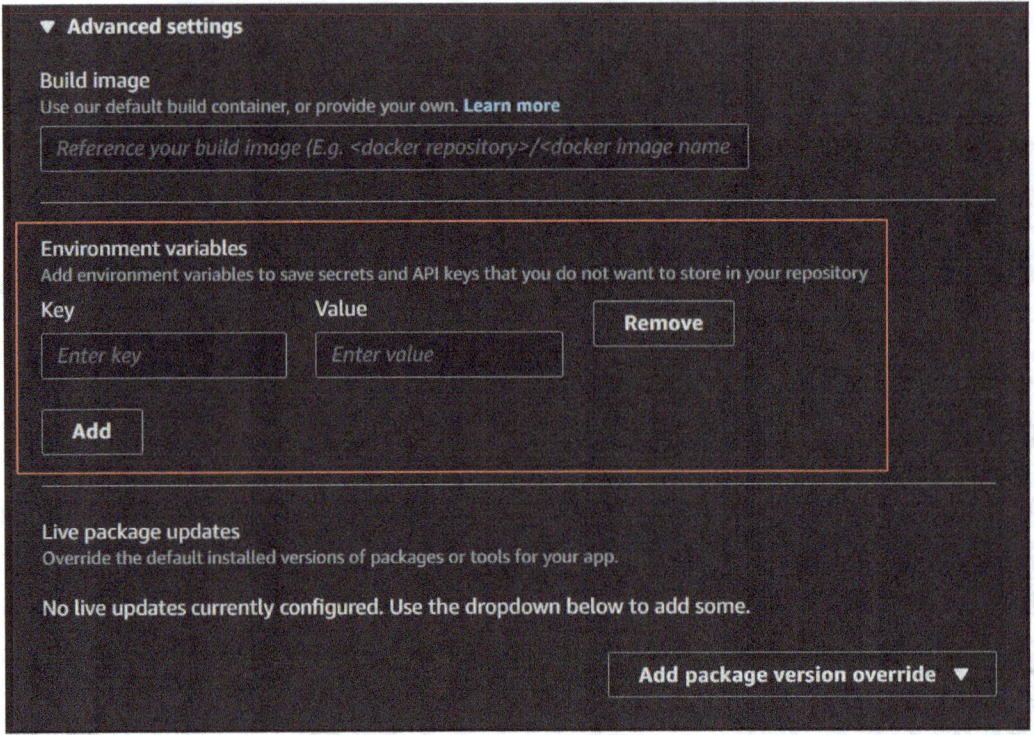

Figure 7.8 – Creating environment variables

8. Now, click on **Next** and, in the next step, review the configurations and click on **Save and deploy**:

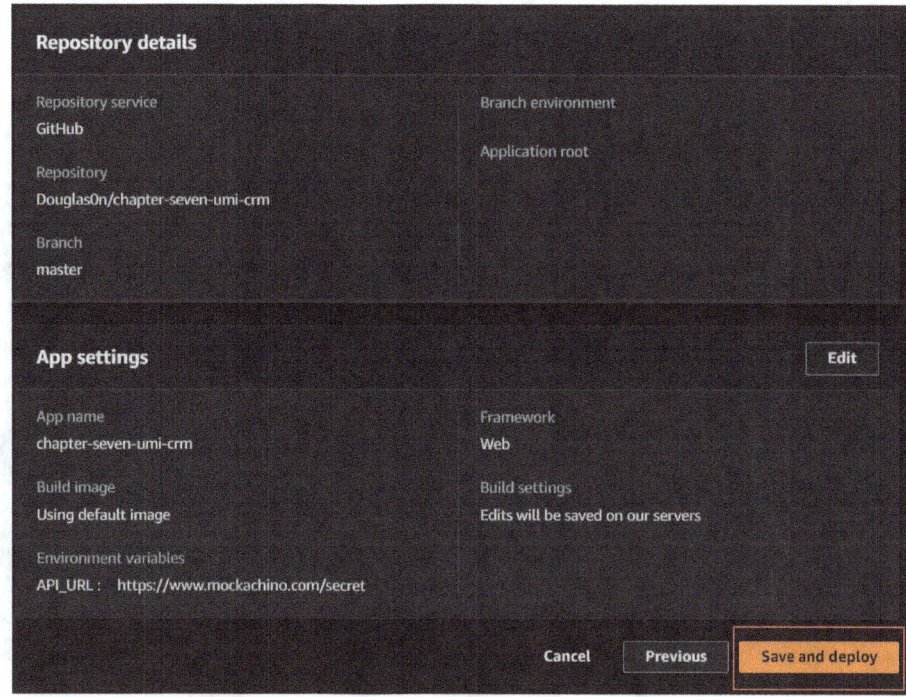

Figure 7.9 – Reviewing and deploying the application

9. Wait for the pipeline to succeed and click on the public address to access the application:

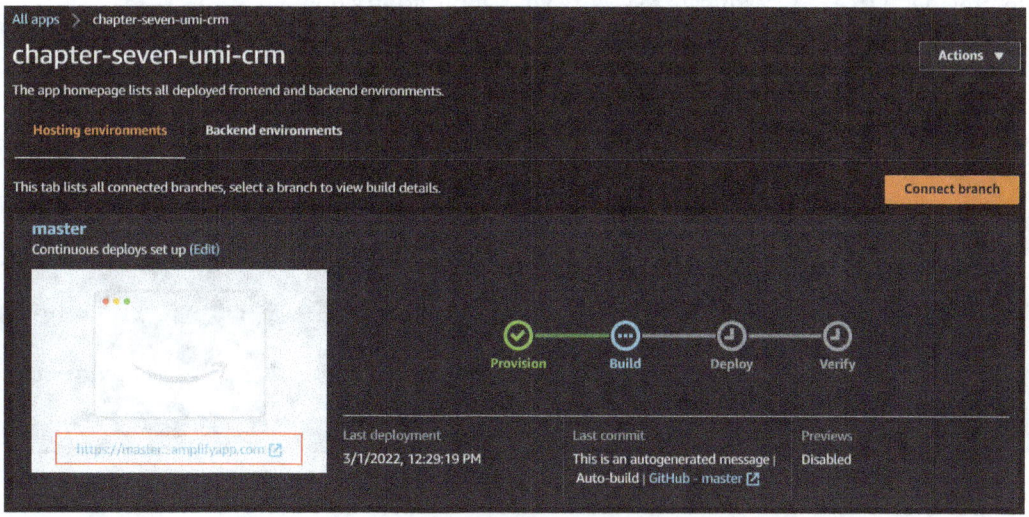

Figure 7.10 – Application public address

Now, let's take a closer look at more Amplify settings.

Understanding more Amplify settings

When hosting a single-page application, it is necessary to configure the server to only respond to requests with the index.html page; otherwise, the server will respond with an error as other pages do not exist on the server.

Amplify provides a default routing rule in the **Rewrites and redirects** configuration. The default rule routes all our application paths to the index.html file.

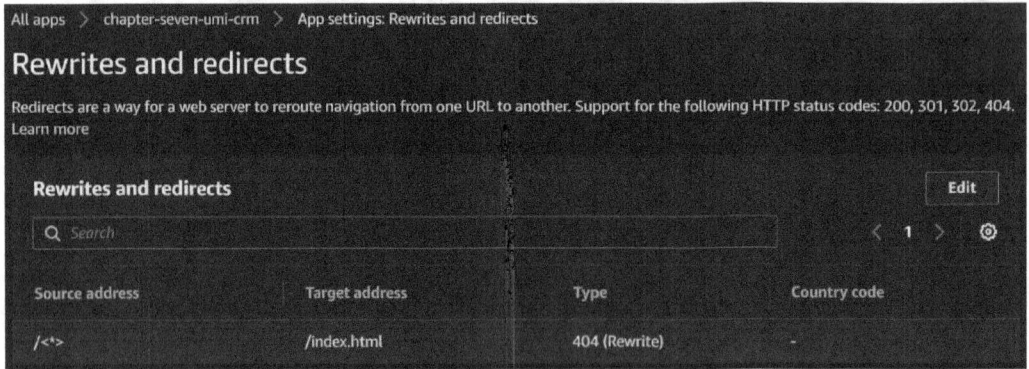

Figure 7.11 – Rewrites and redirects configuration

Amplify also provides a public address on the amplifyapp domain, but you can easily add your custom domain by accessing **Domain management** in the left-side menu.

The domain can be from a hosted zone on AWS Route 53 or other providers, and AWS also provides a free SSL certificate to secure your application's domain.

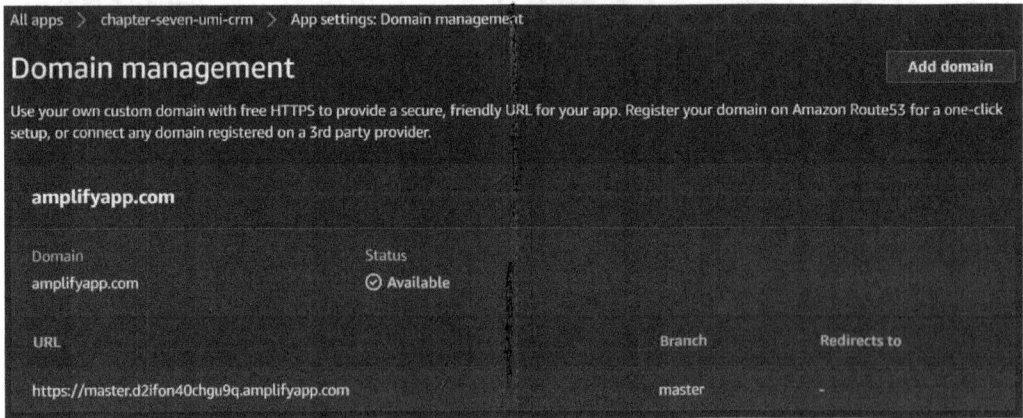

Figure 7.12 – Amplify Domain management

In this section, you created a free AWS account and hosted your application on AWS by connecting Amplify with the repository in your GitHub account. You also learned how to configure rewrites and redirects and manage your custom domain on the Amplify Console.

Summary

In this chapter, we created a mock server for our application using Mockachino, an open source project for quickly mocking servers. You also learned what files Umi generates during the build process for browsers to interpret and render the application. You created an environment variable to define the URL our application will use to send requests.

You learned how to push your application to a repository in your personal GitHub account and created a free AWS account. Next, you hosted your application on AWS by connecting AWS Amplify to your GitHub repository. You also learned how to configure rewrites and redirects, and manage your custom domains on the Amplify Console.

I hope this book has helped you learn how to use UmiJS combined with Ant Design to create robust and professional React applications that provide a great user experience. Keep practicing and exploring the techniques you've learned from this book.

Index

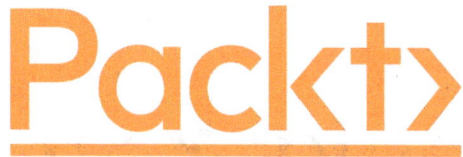

Packt.com

Subscribe to our online digital library for full access to over 7,000 books and videos, as well as industry leading tools to help you plan your personal development and advance your career. For more information, please visit our website.

Why subscribe?

- Spend less time learning and more time coding with practical eBooks and Videos from over 4,000 industry professionals

- Improve your learning with Skill Plans built especially for you

- Get a free eBook or video every month

- Fully searchable for easy access to vital information

- Copy and paste, print, and bookmark content

Did you know that Packt offers eBook versions of every book published, with PDF and ePub files available? You can upgrade to the eBook version at packt.com and as a print book customer, you are entitled to a discount on the eBook copy. Get in touch with us at customercare@packtpub.com for more details.

At www.packt.com, you can also read a collection of free technical articles, sign up for a range of free newsletters, and receive exclusive discounts and offers on Packt books and eBooks.

Other Books You May Enjoy

If you enjoyed this book, you may be interested in these other books by Packt:

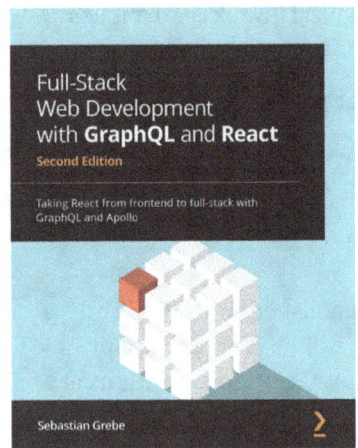

Full-Stack Web Development with GraphQL and React – Second Edition

Sebastian Grebe

ISBN: 978-1-80107-788-0

- Build a GraphQL API by implementing models and schemas with Apollo and Sequelize
- Set up an Apollo Client and build frontend components using React
- Write Reusable React components and use React Hooks
- Authenticate and query user data using GraphQL
- Use Mocha to write test cases for your full-stack application
- Deploy your application to AWS using Docker and CircleCI

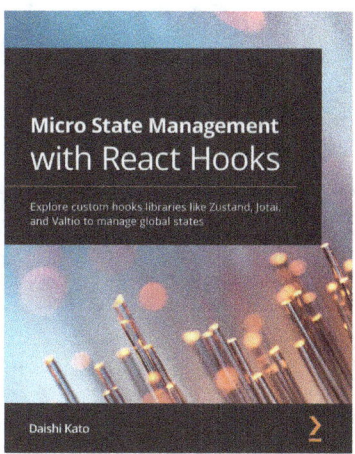

Micro State Management with React Hooks

Daishi Kato

ISBN: 978-1-80181-237-5

- Understand micro state management and how you can deal with global state
- Build libraries using micro state management along with React Hooks
- Discover how micro approaches are easy using React Hooks
- Understand the difference between component state and module state
- Explore several approaches for implementing a global state
- Become well-versed with concrete examples and libraries such as Zustand, Jotai, and Valtio

Packt is searching for authors like you

If you're interested in becoming an author for Packt, please visit `authors.packtpub.com` and apply today. We have worked with thousands of developers and tech professionals, just like you, to help them share their insight with the global tech community. You can make a general application, apply for a specific hot topic that we are recruiting an author for, or submit your own idea.

Hi!

I am Douglas Alves Venancio, author of Enterprise React Development with UmiJS. I really hope you enjoyed reading this book and found it useful for increasing your productivity and efficiency in UmiJS.

It would really help me (and other potential readers!) if you could leave a review on Amazon sharing your thoughts on Enterprise React Development with UmiJS.

Go to the link below or scan the QR code to leave your review:

https://packt.link/r/1803238968

Your review will help me to understand what's worked well in this book, and what could be improved upon for future editions, so it really is appreciated.

Best Wishes,

Douglas Alves Venancio

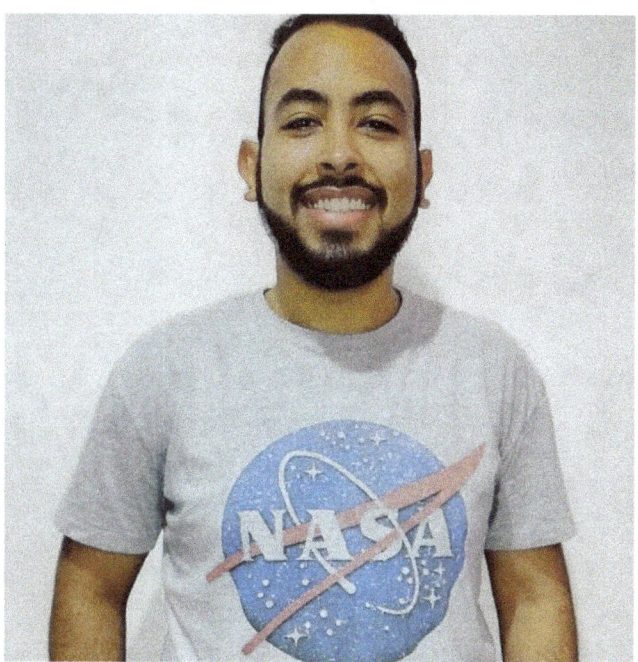